AAT LEVEL 4

Drafting and Interpreting Financial Statements Question Bank

AAT Level 4
Drafting and interpreting
Financial Statements
Question Bank
(Q22 Qb1.4)

Published by Accountext

The content of this pack is frequently updated but on occasion, changes to legislation or accounting standards may not be reflected until sometime after implementation.

The content of this publication is intended to prepare students for AAT examinations and should not be used as professional advice. Accountext Publishing Ltd does not accept any liability for any losses or damage suffered, directly or indirectly, as a result of the information within this text. Professional advice should always be sought.

Accountext Publishing Ltd
First Floor Unit B
Meltex House
65-67 Kepler
Tamworth
B79 7XE

www.accountext.co.uk

Contents

This page is left intentionally blank.

Chapter 1: Background to Financial Accounting

Task 1.1

a) What does IFRS stand for?

	✓
International Financial Reporting Standards	
International Financial Relationship Statistics	
Integrated Financial Reporting Standards	

b) Identify the objective of the IASB from the following options.

	✓
To develop and revise accounting standards in the UK	
To develop a single set of global accounting standards	
To develop and publish local accounting standards in every country	

c) What does GAAP stand for?

	✓
Globally Accepted Accounting Practice	
Generally Accepted Accounting Practice	
Global Accredited Accounting Practices	

d) Identify who issues the international financial reporting standards from the following options.

	✓
The Government	
The International Accounting Standards Board	
The IFRS Foundation	

Task 1.2

Identify if the following statement is true or false.

"The main objective of the Conceptual Framework for Financial Reporting is to provide financial information about the reporting entity that is useful to existing and potential investors, lenders and other creditors in making decisions about providing resources to the entity."

	✓
True	
False	

Task 1.3

Identify from the following the two underlying assumptions recognised by the conceptual framework?

	✓
Relevance	
Going concern	
Faithful representation	
Accruals basis	

Task 1.4

a) What are the two fundamental qualitative characteristics of useful information?

	✓
Timeliness	
Understandability	
Relevance	
Verifiability	
Faithful Representation	
Comparability	

b) What are the four enhancing qualitative characteristics?

	✓
Timeliness	
Understandability	
Relevance	
Verifiability	
Faithful Representation	
Comparability	

Task 1.5

a) Explain the meaning of the term 'relevance' based on the IFRS Conceptual Framework.

b) Explain the meaning of the term 'verifiability' based on the IFRS Conceptual Framework.

Task 1.6

Match the following descriptions to the correct accounting concepts.

Choose from: The business entity concept, Consistency, Materiality, Prudence.

Description	Concept
No information or items should be omitted or misstated that could reasonably impact or influence the decisions of the primary users of the financial statements.	
The financial statements are prepared purely from the perspective of the business – they do not include any valuations of personal assets or liabilities of the owners.	
Adopting a cautious approach when preparing financial statements. Gains or profits should only be recognised in the accounts when they have actually been made, whilst losses should be recorded as soon as it becomes probable they will arise.	
Financial statements should be prepared using the same accounting techniques and valuation bases as previous statements – this is to help make the statements more comparable over time.	

Task 1.7

a) Which key piece of legislation requires limited companies to file annual financial statements?

	✓
The Partnership Act 1890	
The Companies Act 2006	
The Corporate Law Rules 2021	

b) Identify from the following the criteria that must be met for a limited company to be exempt from being audited.

	✓
An annual turnover of no more than £10.2 million	
An annual turnover of no more than £8 million	
Assets worth no more than £5.1 million	
50 or fewer employees on average	
Assets worth no more than £7 million	

c) Identify which of the following must be presented by limited companies.

	✓
A Statement of Profit or Loss and Other Comprehensive Income	
A Statement of Changes in Equity	
A Statement of Financial Position	
A Statement of Cash Flows	
A Directors' Report	
Appropriation Account	
Group (Consolidated) Accounts where a company has subsidiaries	
Capital Accounts	

Task 1.8

State what information each of the following financial statements provides for users.

Statement of Profit or Loss and Other Comprehensive Income

Statement of Financial Position

Statement of Cash Flows

Statement of Changes in Equity

Task 1.9

a) What are the elements of the Statement of Financial Position?

	✓
Assets	
Expenses	
Sales	
Equity	
Liabilities	
Purchases	

b) What is the accounting equation that the Statement of Financial position is based on?

	=		+	

Task 1.10

The conceptual framework defines the five elements of the financial statements.

Write the definitions of each element in the spaces below.

Definition of an Asset

Definition of a Liability

Definition of Equity

Definition of Income

Definition of Expense

Chapter 2: Financial Statements of Limited Companies

Task 2.1

Identify which of the following businesses are unincorporated or incorporated.

	Unincorporated / Incorporated
Sole trader	
Private limited company	
Limited liability partnership	
Public limited company	
Partnership	

Task 2.2

Identify which of the following statements are true.

	✓
Sole traders have limited liability and their personal assets are not assets at risk.	
Shareholders have limited liability and are only liable to lose the amount they originally invested if the business fails.	
Sole traders and partners take dividends from the profits of the business.	
Shareholders appoint directors for the day to day running of the business.	
Limited companies pay Corporation Tax on their profits and must file a copy of their financial statements to Companies House each year.	
Directors cannot also be shareholders of a company.	
Public limited companies can offer shares to the general public to raise capital.	

Task 2.3

There are some key differences in the way in which the financial statements are produced for limited companies compare with Sole traders and Partnerships.

Identify which of the following relate to limited companies only.

	✓
Owners are not involved in the day-to-day management of the business.	
Filing annual financial statements at companies house every year is not required.	
Annual financial statements must be prepared in line with the accounting standards.	
The owners' *equity* is made up of the amounts they have originally invested, retained earnings and other gains and losses.	
Limited companies pay corporation tax on their profits.	
The owners of the business will take money out of the business through drawings.	

Task 2.4

Match each of the following stakeholders to whether they are internal or external.

Stakeholder	Internal ✓	External ✓
Investors		
Managers		
Lenders		
Shareholders		
Staff		
The Government		
Local communities		
Customers / Suppliers		

Task 2.5

Describe three main differences between the financial statements of sole traders and limited companies?

Task 2.6

A company has calculated the value of its closing inventories at the year end at £450,000. It has subsequently realised that goods included in this figure which had been valued at £40,000 were in fact only able to sold for £10,000 due to damage.

What is the revised value of the inventory for inclusion in the Statement of Financial Position at the year end?

£

Task 2.7

Identify which of the following items would be shown in the Statement of Profit or Loss and Other comprehensive Income or the Statement of Financial Position.

	In SPLOCI	In SFP
Ordinary Share Capital		
Share Premium Reserve		
Revaluation Reserve		
Administrative Expenses		
Trade and Other Payables		
Retained earnings		
Distribution Costs		
Land and buildings – at cost		
Plant and equipment – at cost		
Land and buildings – accumulated depreciation		
Plant and equipment – accumulated depreciation		
Trade and Other Receivables		
Accruals		
Prepayments		
Bank Loan		
Interest Paid		
Sales		
Purchases		
Inventories at start of the year		
Sales Returns		
Purchase Returns		
Provision for Doubtful Debts		
Final Dividend		
Cash & Cash Equivalents		
Inventories at the end of the year		
Tax charge for the year		
Interim Dividend		

Task 2.8

Fusion-Tech Ltd

You have been asked to help with the preparation of the financial statements of Fusion-Tech Ltd for the year ended 30 November 20X3.

The company's trial balance as at 30 November 20X3 is as follows:

	£000	£000
Share Capital		6,000
Trade and Other Payables		2,526
Administrative Expenses	2,687	
Retained earnings at 1 December 20X6		6,784
Distribution Costs	3,987	
Sales		27,623
Plant and equipment – at cost	36,841	
Purchases	15,664	
Plant and equipment – accumulated depreciation		18,250
Trade and Other Receivables	3,660	
6% Loan Repayable 20X7		8,200
Accruals		233
Interest paid	246	
Cash & Cash Equivalents	1,166	
Inventories at 1 December 20X2	4,245	
Dividends Paid	1,120	
	69,616	69,616

Further information:

- The inventories at the close of business on the 30 November 20X3 cost £5,274,000.
- Credit sales for the whole of November have not been included. The total to be added is £2,250,000. Ignore any VAT.
- The tax charge for the year has been calculated as £934,000.
- Only six months of the interest on the bank loan has been included in the trial balance. The remaining six months of interest has not yet been paid.
- Included within the administrative expenses in the trial balance is £27,000 which relates to indemnity insurance. This was paid in July 20X3. This payment covers one year's insurance from 1 August 20X3 to 31 July 20X4.

a) Draft the statement of profit or loss and other comprehensive income for Fusion-Tech Ltd for the year ended 30 November 20X3.

b) Draft the statement of financial position for Fusion-Tech Ltd as at 30 November 20X3. Use the workings boxes to help you.

Fusion-Tech Ltd Statement of Profit or Loss and Other Comprehensive Income for the year ended 30 November 20X3	
	£000
Revenue	
Cost of Sales	
Gross profit	
Distribution Costs	
Administrative Expenses	
Operating profit	
Finance Costs	
Profit before tax	
Tax	
Profit for the period from continuing operations	
Other Comprehensive Income	
Total comprehensive income for the year	

Workings boxes:

Cost of Sales	£000
Opening Inventories	
Purchases	
Closing Inventories	
Total	

Administrative Expenses	£000
Administrative expenses	
Prepayment	
Total	

Fusion-Tech Ltd Statement of Financial Position as at 30 November 20X3	
	£000
ASSETS	
Non-Current Assets	
Property, Plant and Equipment	
Current Assets	
Inventories	
Trade and Other Receivables	
Cash and Cash Equivalents	
TOTAL ASSETS	
EQUITY AND LIABILITIES	
Equity	
Share Capital	
Retained Earnings	
Total Equity	
Non-current Liabilities	
Bank loans	
Current Liabilities	
Trade and Other Payables	
Tax Payable	
Total Liabilities	
TOTAL EQUITY AND LIABILITIES	

Workings boxes:

Trade and Other Receivables	£000
Trade and other receivables	
Prepayment	
Credit sales	
Total	

Retained Earnings	£000
Retained earnings	
Profit for the year	
Dividends paid	
Total	

Trade and Other Payables	£000
Trade and other payables	
Accruals	
Interest accrual	
Total	

Task 2.9

Eco-Verse Ltd

You have been asked to help with the preparation of the financial statements of Eco-Verse Ltd for the year ended 31 October 20X2.

The company's trial balance as at 31 October 20X2 is as follows:

Trial Balance	£000	£000
Share Capital		15,000
Trade and Other Payables		2,894
Administrative Expenses	2,945	
Retained earnings at 1 November 20X1		3,926
Land and buildings	25,200	
Land and buildings accumulated depreciation at 1 November 20X1		4,000
Plant & Equipment – at cost	13,250	
Plant & Equipment – accumulated depreciation at 1 November 20X1		3,800
Distribution costs	2,834	
Trade and Other Receivables	3,098	
8% Loan Repayable 20X6		9,000
Accruals		282
Interest	360	
Cash & Cash Equivalents	5,280	
Inventories at 1 November 20X1	4,586	
Dividends Paid	1,300	
Sales		38,201
Purchases	18,250	
	77,103	**77,103**

Further information:

- The inventories at the close of business on 31 October 20X2 were valued at £3,939,000.
- Depreciation is to be provided for the year to 31 October 20X2 as follows:

Buildings	2% per annum	Straight line basis
Plant and equipment	20% per annum	Diminishing balance

  Depreciation should be apportioned as follows:

Cost of Sales	60%
Distribution costs	20%
Administrative expenses	20%

- Land, which is non-depreciable, is included in the trial balance at a cost of £8,200,000.
- The company began a series of television adverts for the company's new product on 1 October 20X2 at a cost of £27,000. The adverts were to run for three months and were to be paid for in full at the end of December 20X2. Advertising expenses have been included in distribution costs.
- Interest on the bank loan for the last six months of the year have not been included in the accounts in the trial balance.
- The corporation tax charge for the year has been calculated as £1,520,000.

a) Draft the statement of profit or loss and other comprehensive income for Eco-Verse Ltd for the year ended year ended 31 October 20X2.

b) Draft the statement of financial position for Eco-Verse Ltd year ended 31 October 20X2.

Use the workings boxes to help you.

Eco-Verse Ltd Statement of Profit or Loss and Other Comprehensive Income for the year ended 31 October 20X2	
	£000
Gross profit	
Operating profit	
Profit before tax	
Profit for the period from continuing operations	
Total comprehensive income for the year	

Workings boxes:

Cost of Sales	£000
Opening Inventories	
Purchases	
Closing Inventories	
Depreciation	
Total	

Distribution Costs	£000
Distribution Costs	
Depreciation	
Accruals	
Total	

Administrative Expenses	£000
Administrative expenses	
Depreciation	
Total	

Eco-Verse Ltd Statement of Financial Position as at 31 October 20X2	
	£000
ASSETS	
Non-Current Assets	
Current Assets	
TOTAL ASSETS	
EQUITY AND LIABILITIES	
Equity	
Total Equity	
Non-current Liabilities	
Current Liabilities	
Total Liabilities	
TOTAL EQUITY AND LIABILITIES	

Workings boxes:

PPE	£000
Land and buildings at cost	
Accumulated depreciation – land and buildings	
Plant and equipment at cost	
Accumulated depreciation of plant and equipment	
Total	

Retained Earnings	£000
Retained earnings	
Profit for the year	
Dividends paid	
Total	

Trade and Other Payables	£000
Trade and other payables	
Accruals (from TB)	
Distribution accrual	
Interest accrual	
Total	

Task 2.10

Dickinson Distribution Ltd

You have been asked to help with the preparation of the financial statements of Dickinson Distribution Ltd for the year ended 31 December 20X4.

The company's trial balance as at 31 December 20X4 is as follows:

Trial Balance	£000	£000
Share Capital		5,000
Trade and Other Payables		965
Administrative Expenses	982	
Retained earnings at 1 January 20X4		1,309
Land and buildings	8,400	
Land and buildings accumulated depreciation at 1 January 20X4		1,333
Plant & Equipment – at cost	4,417	
Plant & Equipment – accumulated depreciation at 1 January 20X4		1,267
Distribution costs	945	
Trade and Other Receivables	1,033	
8% Loan Repayable 20X9		3,000
Accruals		94
Interest	120	
Cash & Cash Equivalents	1,760	
Inventories at 1 January 20X4	1,529	
Dividends Paid	433	
Sales		12,734
Purchases	6,083	
	25,702	**25,702**

Further information:

- The inventories at the close of business on 31 December 20X4 were valued at £1,313,000.
- Depreciation is to be provided for the year to 31 December 20X4 as follows:

Buildings	5% per annum	Straight line basis
Plant and equipment	20% per annum	Diminishing balance

  Depreciation should be apportioned as follows:

Cost of Sales	40%
Distribution costs	40%
Administrative expenses	20%

- Land, which is non-depreciable, is included in the trial balance at a cost of £2,700,000.
- Trade receivables include a debt of £45,000 which is to be written off. Irrecoverable debts are charged to administrative expenses.
- Interest on the bank loan for the last six months of the year have not been included in the accounts in the trial balance.
- The corporation tax charge for the year has been calculated as £308,000.

a) Draft the statement of profit or loss and other comprehensive income for Dickinson Distribution Ltd for the year ended year ended 31 December 20X4.

b) Draft the statement of financial position for Dickinson Distribution Ltd year ended 31 December 20X4.

Use the workings boxes to help you.

Dickinson Distribution Ltd Statement of Profit or Loss and Other Comprehensive Income for the year ended 31 December 20X4	
	£000
Gross profit	
Operating profit	
Profit before tax	
Profit for the period from continuing operations	
Total comprehensive income for the year	

Workings boxes:

Cost of Sales	£000
Total	

Administrative Expenses	£000
Total	

Distribution Costs	£000
Total	

Dickinson Distribution Ltd Statement of Financial Position as at 31 October 20X2	
	£000
ASSETS	
Non-Current Assets	
Current Assets	
TOTAL ASSETS	
EQUITY AND LIABILITIES	
Equity	
Total Equity	
Non-current Liabilities	
Current Liabilities	
Total Liabilities	
TOTAL EQUITY AND LIABILITIES	

Workings boxes:

PPE	£000
Total	

Trade and Other Receivables	£000
Total	

Retained Earnings	£000
Total	

Trade and Other Payables	£000
Total	

This page is left intentionally blank.

Chapter 3: Equity

Task 3.1

a) Identify the correct items that are included in the 'Equity' section of the Statement of Financial Position for limited companies.

	✓
Share capital	
Capital account	
Revaluation reserve	
Retained earnings	
Share premium	
Assets	

b) Identify the two major classes of shares in limited companies from the following options.

	✓
Ordinary shares	
Selection shares	
Possession shares	
Preference shares	

Task 3.2

a) Explain what is meant by the term 'bonus shares'.

b) Explain what is meant by the term 'rights issue' in relation to shares.

Task 3.3

Marine Manufacturing Ltd issued 10,000 shares for £1.50 each. The nominal value of the shares is 50p.

a) Calculate the amount to be entered in the share capital account and the share premium account.

Share Capital:	£	
Share Premium:	£	

b) What would be the account treatment for this?

Account name	Dr or Cr	Amount
Cash received (bank)		
Share capital		
Share premium		

Task 3.4

N&S Plc has made a bonus issue of new £1 ordinary shares to its existing shareholders. N&S Plc has offered the bonus issue on a 1:4 basis, using the share premium account. The offer is accepted by all existing shareholders.

Before the bonus issue there were 10,000 ordinary £1 issued shares. The share premium reserve balance was £7,000. The retained earnings of the company were £128,000.

a) Calculate the total number of issued shares after the bonus issue.

Original issue = ________________

Bonus Issue = ________________

Total = ________________

b) Show the double entry to record the bonus issue.

	Account	£
Dr		
Cr		

c) Complete the equity section of the Statement of Financial Position.

Equity (extract)	
Ordinary shares	
Share premium	
Retained earnings	
Total equity	

Task 3.5

Katerina Catering Ltd has property that has been revalued and it has increased in value. This must be recognised in the accounts of the business. Identify whether the following entries will be a debit or credit to record this increase.

	DR / CR
Property at cost	
Accumulated depreciation	
Revaluation reserve	

Task 3.6

A company made a share issue during the year of 160,000 ordinary £1 shares, raising £260,000. How is this shown in the Statement of Changes in Equity?

	✓
It should not be recorded in the Statement of Changes in Equity.	
Include £260,000 in Share Capital.	
Include £160,000 in Share Capital and £100,000 in Revaluation Reserve.	
Include £160,000 in Share Capital and £100,000 in Share Premium Reserve.	

Task 3.7

a) Complete the following sentence.

Any profits not paid out in the form of dividends are called ____________________.

b) Calculate the retained earnings to be included in the Statement of Financial position for the year ended 31 December 20X4.

Retained Earnings	£000
Retained earnings at 1 Jan 20X4	1,234
Profit for the period	840
Dividends paid	650
Retained earnings at 31 December 20X4	

Task 3.8

Palmers Ltd has had a property revalued. The cost of the property was originally £10 Million. It has been revalued at £16 million. The accumulated depreciation is currently £2.5 million.

What would the double entry be to record this?

Account	Dr or Cr	Amount
Property at cost		
Accumulated Depreciation		
Revaluation reserve		

Task 3.9

In the year ended 31st December 20X4, Boardman Ltd made an operating profit after tax of £630,000. During the year the following events occurred:

- There was a revaluation of freehold properties owned by the company, resulting in a gain of £250,000.
- The company issued 60,000 new £1 ordinary shares, raising £100,000 new capital.
- A dividend of £300,000 was made to shareholders.

Equity balances as at 1st January 20X4 were:

Share Capital	£300,000
Share Premium	£70,000
Revaluation Reserve	£ 0
Retained Profits	£285,000

Prepare the Statement of Changes in Equity for the year ended 31st December 20X4.

	Share Capital	Share Premium	Revaluation Reserve	Retained Earnings	Total Equity
	£000	£000	£000	£000	£000
Balance at start of year					
Changes in Equity:					
Comprehensive Income					
Dividends					
Issue of Share Capital					
Balance at end of year					

Task 3.10

Sharp Manufacturing Ltd

You have been asked to help with the preparation of the financial statements of Sharp Manufacturing Ltd for the year ended 31 December 20X4.

The company's trial balance as at 31 December 20X4 is as follows:

	£000	£000
Trade and Other Receivables	746	
Trade and Other Payables		705
Prepayments	89	
Cash at bank	61	
Bank loan repayable in 20X9		985
Share capital (£1 ordinary shares)		3,564
Retained earnings at 1st January 20X1		703
Property, plant & equipment cost	9,198	
Property plant & equipment accumulated depreciation		4,106
Sales		9,629
Sales returns	35	
Purchases	5,818	
Purchases returns		47
Distribution costs	812	
Administrative expenses	1,601	
Inventories at 1st January 20X1	1,034	
Interest paid	70	
Dividends paid	275	
	19,739	**19,739**

Further information:

- The inventories at the close of business on the 31 December 20X4 cost £925,000.
- An invoice for £24,000 in respect of marketing costs for the period 1 November 20X4 to 31 January 20X5 was received on 5th February 20X5. The invoice was not included in the balances in the trial balance. Marketing costs are treated as a distribution cost.
- A salary of £55,000 paid to the senior manager of the distribution warehouse has been incorrectly classified as an administrative expense.
- The corporation tax charge in respect of the profits for the current year of 31 December 20X4 has been estimated at £231,000.
- Trade receivables include a debt of £26,000 that is to be written off. Irrecoverable debts are classified as an administrative expense.

a) Draft the statement of profit or loss and other comprehensive income for Sharp Manufacturing Ltd for the year ended 31 December 20X4.

b) Draft the statement of financial position for Sharp Manufacturing Ltd as at 31 December 20X4.

Sharp Manufacturing Ltd Statement of Profit or Loss and Other Comprehensive Income for the year ended 31 December 20X4	
	£000
Revenue	
Cost of Sales	
Gross profit	
Distribution Costs	
Administrative Expenses	
Operating profit	
Finance Costs	
Profit before tax	
Tax	
Profit for the period from continuing operations	
Other Comprehensive Income	
Total comprehensive income for the year	

Workings boxes:

Cost of Sales	£000
Opening Inventories	
Purchases	
Closing Inventories	
Total	

Administrative Expenses	£000
Administrative expenses	
Salary	
Irrecoverable debt	
Total	

Distribution Costs	£000
Distribution Costs	
Accrual	
Salary	
Total	

Sharp Manufacturing Ltd Statement of Financial Position as at 31 December 20X4	
	£000
ASSETS	
Non-Current Assets	
Property, Plant and Equipment	
Current Assets	
Inventories	
Trade and Other Receivables	
Cash and Cash Equivalents	
TOTAL ASSETS	
EQUITY AND LIABILITIES	
Equity	
Share Capital	
Retained Earnings	
Total Equity	
Non-current Liabilities	
Bank loans	
Current Liabilities	
Trade and Other Payables	
Tax Payable	
Total Liabilities	
TOTAL EQUITY AND LIABILITIES	

Workings boxes:

Trade and Other Receivables	£000
Trade and other receivables	
Prepayment	
Irrecoverable debt	
Total	

Retained Earnings	£000
Retained earnings	
Profit for the year	
Dividends paid	
Total	

Trade and Other Payables	£000
Trade and other payables	
Accruals	
Total	

c) Draft the Statement of Changes in Equity for Sharp Manufacturing Ltd as at 31 December 20X4.

	Share Capital	Revaluation Surplus	Retained Earnings	Total Equity
	£000	£000	£000	£000
Balance at start of year				
Changes in Equity:				
Comprehensive Income				
Dividends				
Issue of Share Capital				
Balance at end of year				

This page is left intentionally blank.

Chapter 4: Assets

Task 4.1

a) Identify which of the following are current or non-current assets.

Assets	Current / Non-current
Trade receivables	
Prepayments	
Land	
Vehicles	
Cash and cash equivalents	
Inventories	
Plant and machinery	
Office equipment	

b) Identify which of the following are characteristics of a non-current asset.

	✓
Must be tangible	
Can be tangible and intangible	
Is expected to be used over more than one period of 12 months	
Is expected to be used within one period of 12 months	

c) Identify which International Accounting Standard deals with the tangible assets of Plant, Property and Equipment.

	✓
IAS 2	
IAS 16	
IAS 36	
IAS 37	

Task 4.2

a) Identify which of the following IAS 16 considers when dealing with non-current assets.

	✓
Impairment of assets	
When to recognise an asset	
How to record the carrying value of an asset	
How to record leased assets	
When and how to depreciate non-current assets	
Intangible assets	

b) Which two criteria must be met when identifying whether an asset should be recognised in the financial statements?

1.
2.

c) Companies are permitted to value their assets on two bases. Identify which model the following descriptions relate to.

	Model
Where non-current assets are revalued periodically, and revalued at their 'fair value' less any subsequent accumulated depreciation.	
Where non-current assets are valued at their historic cost, less accumulated depreciation.	

d) Identify which of the following statements is **false**.

	✓
If an entity chooses to adopt the revaluation model, then all assets in the same class must be valued using this basis.	
If an entity chooses to adopt the revaluation model, then only that particular asset must be valued using this basis.	
Under the revaluation model, assets of that class must be revalued regularly to ensure the carrying amount of the asset does not materially differ from its fair value stated in the financial statements.	
If an entity chooses to adopt the revaluation model for a class of asset, then other classes of assets can continue to use the cost model.	

Task 4.3

a) Where an asset is revalued upwards, what are the accounting entries to record this?

DR
CR

b) Where would this appear in the financial statements?

	✓
Increase Non-Current Assets (SFP)	
Other Comprehensive Income (SPL)	
Revenue as additional income (SPL)	
Equity section (SFP)	
Non-Current Liabilities (SFP)	

c) Which of the following costs could be included in the cost of a new industrial drilling machine?

a) Costs of site preparation.

b) Costs of testing the asset before being brought into use.

c) Cost of professional fees (e.g. architect or surveyor).

d) Cost of ongoing maintenance contract for the machine.

e) Cost of initial delivery of the machine.

f) Cost of replacement drill pieces for the machine.

d) The company purchased a new machine on 1st January 20X1 for use in the production process at a cost of £200,000. The machine has an estimated useful life of 5 years and a residual value of £10,000.

Calculate the depreciation expense recognised in the Statement of Profit of Loss and the carrying amount of the asset to be recorded in the Statement of Financial Position as at 31st December 20X3 using:

i) Straight line method.

	Depreciation for the year (SPL)	Carrying Amount (SFP)
31/12/20X1		
31/12/20X2		
31/12/20X3		

ii) Diminishing / reducing balance method at 20% per annum.

	Depreciation for the year (SPL)	Carrying Amount (SFP
31/12/20X1		
31/12/20X2		
31/12/20X3		

Task 4.4

a) Complete the following sentences.

Choose from: controls, lease, Lessee, Lessor, right of use, own.

A business does not necessarily have to ______ an item for it to be considered an asset; it may be enough that it simply __________ the item.

A lease contract is an agreement between the __________ (who owns the asset) and the ____________ (who leases the asset).

The lessee has the ________________ of the asset in exchange for payment made to the lessor.

b) Is the following statement true or false?

A contract is, or contains, a lease if it conveys the right to control the use of an identified asset for the period of time in exchange for consideration.

	✓
True	
False	

c) Complete the following sentences.

Choose from: past, present, current, increase, decrease, completely, partially.

A lease liability will be recognised at the _____________ value of the minimum lease payments. This liability will then _____________ over the lease period until it has been ________________ repaid by the end of the agreement.

Task 4.5

Axel Ltd is a parts manufacturer. In Axel Ltd's latest financial year, it entered a number of lease agreements for assets as below. For each, you should identify whether it should be treated as a **short term lease, low value asset lease** or a **lease**.

Leases	Type
Leased a packing machine on a 10 month lease. The value of the machine is £7,000.	
Leased a van for making small deliveries on a three year lease. The list price of the van at the time of the lease is £16,000. The lease payments are agreed at £460 per month for the duration of the lease.	
Leased a machine on a four year contract. At the end of the four-year period Axel Ltd will own the asset.	
Leased a photocopier / printer. The term of the lease is 2 years and the value of the printer is £1,500.	

Task 4.6

Mason Engineering Ltd have leased a machine with a lease term of 4 years. The commencement date is 1 January 20X3. The asset has a useful life of 10 years. Lease payments are £10,000 per year. With the first payment being due on the 1 January 20X3. The present value has already been calculated as £37,230. Mason Engineering Ltd will own the asset at the end of the lease term.

The interest rate implicit on the lease is 5%.

What entries will be entered into the Statement of Profit or Loss at the end of the year. Round your answers to the nearest whole pound.

Entry	£	Workings

Identify the entries to be entered into the Statement of Financial Position at the end of the year?

Entry	£	Workings

How will the lease liability be split between the non-current liabilities and the current liabilities in the Statement of Financial Position?

	£

Task 4.7

At the start of the financial year Rhymes Rotors Ltd entered a lease agreement for seven new vans for a period of four years. A photocopier was also leased for the main office. The agreement relating to the photocopier is for twelve months. This is the first time that Rhymes Rotors Ltd has had any lease agreements. They are unsure of the correct accounting treatment and have asked for your advice.

a) Identify the relevant accounting standard and an explanation on how they will need to be treated these in the financial statements.

On the 1 April 20X6 Vanguard Ltd entered into a 4 year lease for new plant machinery. They will pay 4 annual payments of £8,000 per year. The first payment is due on the 31 March 20X7. The rate implicit on the lease is 6%. The present value of the lease payments has been calculated as £29,384.

b) Explain how the lease should be recognised in the financial statements of Vanguard Ltd for the year ended 31 March 20X7. Show your calculations to illustrate your answer.

Task 4.8

a) Identify which International Accounting Standard deals with the impairment of assets.

	✓
IAS 2	
IAS 16	
IAS 36	
IAS 37	

b) One of the machines owned by the company has been damaged and might have become impaired.

Details of the value of the machine are as follows:

Carry Amount	£54,000
Fair Value	£45,600
Cost of Disposal	£4,800
Value in Use	£43,200

What amount should be recognised for the machine in the Statement of Financial Position?

What is the amount of impairment loss that will be recognised in the Statement of Profit or Loss?

c) The company owns three assets. Due to a fire at the factory, there is concern that some of these assets may have become impaired.

The following information is available:

Asset	Carrying Amount	Fair value less costs to sell	Value in use
1	25,000	26,000	22,500
2	37,500	34,000	31,500
3	75,000	37,500	65,000

Which of the assets have become impaired?

i) 1
ii) 2
iii) 1 and 2
iv) 1 and 3
v) 2 and 3

What is the impairment amount to be included in the Statement of Profit or Loss?

Task 4.9

a) Identify which of the following best describes an intangible asset under IAS 38.

	✓
An identifiable, non-monetary asset without physical form.	
An identifiable, monetary asset with physical form.	

b) Complete the following sentences.

Choose from: depreciation, discretion, accumulation, definite, indefinite.

Amortisation is the same as ____________, however amortisation only applies to intangible assets.

Intangible assets with a ____________useful life are subject to amortisation. Intangible assets with an ______________ useful life are not subject to amortisation but instead are reviewed annually for impairment.

c) Identify which of the following are examples of intangible assets.

	✓
Goodwill	
Inventory	
Development costs	
Trade marks, licences, patents	
Computer equipment	
Vehicles	

d) Identify which of the following statements are true.

	✓
Internally generated brands cannot be recognised as an intangible asset because they cannot be measured reliably.	
Intangible assets which meet the recognition criteria should never be shown in the Statement of Financial Position.	
Intangible assets which meet the recognition criteria should be shown in the Statement of Financial Position at their original cost.	
Indefinite life intangible assets are not amortised, instead they are reviewed for impairment and if a finite life can be established.	
Intangible assets with an indefinite life must be amortised over that life on a systematic basis.	

Swanson Supplies Ltd is a large company that spends a lot of money in research and development. Danica (a colleague) has emailed you asking for some advice. She has asked whether or not she should capitalise some recent research and development expenditure and she is unsure of what the criteria is.

Write a short email to Danica and outline what the criteria is for development expenditure to be capitalised in accordance with IAS 38 Intangible Assets.

Task 4.10

a) Identify from the following what inventories must be valued at, under IAS 2.

	✓
The higher of cost and net realisable value.	
The lower of cost and net realisable value.	
The higher of the indirect cost and incurred cost.	
The lower of present value and original cost.	

b) Identify from the following which costs should be included in the cost of inventories?

	✓
Selling costs	
Transportation costs to the warehouse	
Import costs	
Storage and distribution costs	

c) Calculate the value of the inventory be stated as in the financial statements according to IAS 2 Inventories.

Product	FIFO	LIFO	NRV
T100	25,000	24,900	28,500
Y300	16,600	16,200	16,400
Z500	35,800	34,500	36,200
Total	**77,400**	**75,600**	**81,100**

£

d) The business sells the following three products.

	Cost	Selling Costs	Selling Price
C3	27,000	4,080	30,240
F5	51,840	960	53,040
H6	39,120	2,640	42,240

In accordance with IAS 2 Inventories, what is the value of the closing inventories to be recognised in the financial statements?

£

Chapter 5: Other Accounting Standards

Task 5.1

a) Select the correct international accounting standard that deals with events after the reporting period.

	✓
IAS 2	
IAS 16	
IAS 10	
IAS 37	

Task 5.2

Complete the following sentences.

Choose from: adjust, IAS 10, IAS 38, events, impact, reporting, time.

There is a 'window' of time between when the ______________ period has ended and when the financial statements have been finalised and authorised.

During this time ________ could occur that could have an __________ on the information contained within those financial statements.

_______ provides guidance on when an entity should ________ its financial statements for events after the reporting period.

Task 5.3

Identify which of the following best describes a material adjusting event and a material non-adjusting event.

Description	Adjusting / Non-adjusting
Is accounted for by altering the amounts shown in the financial statements to reflect the event.	
Is not included by amending the financial statements. Instead, it is included as a note to the accounts giving, where possible, an indication of the likely financial effect of the event.	

Task 5.4

Ramana Ltd is preparing its financial statements to 31st December 20X4. The following events occurred in January 20X5, before the financial statements had been authorised.

Identify from the following which are adjusting events and non-adjusting events.

Events	Adjusting / Non-adjusting
Damage to non-current assets or loss of production due to fire or flood.	
Impairment of assets.	
A reduction in value of inventories where net realisable value falls below cost.	
Issue of new share capital.	
Discovery of fraud by an employee.	
The major purchase of non-current assets.	
Conclusion of a court case which had been ongoing at the financial year end.	
A new business combination – purchase of, or sale to, another entity.	
Insolvency of a major trade customer.	
Taking out a new (or increasing an existing) loan.	

Task 5.5

On 1st April 20X4, Centurion Ltd had an estimated corporation tax liability of £85,000 in respect of the financial year ended 31st March 20X4.

In August 20X4, Centurion Ltd paid £75,000 to HMRC in respect of the corporation tax liability for the year ended 31st March 20X4.

At 31st March 20X5 Centurion Ltd estimate their tax liability for the financial year 20X4-X5 to be £100,000.

a) Identify if there has been an over provision or an under provision for the year ended 31 March 20X4.

	✓
Over provision	
Under provision	

b) Calculate the tax charge that Centurion Ltd will show in the Statement of Profit or Loss and Other Comprehensive Income for the year ended 31st March 20X5.

£

c) Calculate the tax liability that will be shown in the Statement of Financial Position as at the 31 March 20X5.

£

Task 5.6

Allure Ltd is preparing it financial statements for the year ended 31 December 20X8. The corporation tax charge on profits for the current year was estimated at £32,000. In the previous year, Allure Ltd under-estimated its corporation tax liability by £5,000.

Calculate the amount that should be included in the statement of profit or loss for the year ended 31 December 20X8.

£

Task 5.7

The management of Goldstar Ltd are looking to start preparing the financial statements for the year ended 30 May 20X3.

Sales for the year to 31 March 20X3 include deposits from customers totalling £24,500. The deposits relate to products which are currently in the process of being manufactured and will not be received by the customers until July 20X3.

The management of Goldstar Ltd are unsure of the accounting treatment of the revenue here.

Identify the relevant accounting standard that needs to be applied and how this should be recognised in the financial statements.

Task 5.8

a) Identify the accounting treatment for contingent liabilities based on the likelihood of the event occurring. Choose from: Make provision, disclose in notes or ignore.

Event	Treatment
Almost certain	
Probable	
Possible	
Remote	

b) Identify the accounting treatment for contingent assets based on the likelihood of the event occurring. Choose from: Recognise, disclose in notes or ignore.

Event	Treatment
Almost certain	
Probable	
Possible	
Remote	

c) Identify if the following statements are true or false.

Event	True / False
A contingent asset is never shown in the financial statements if it is probable the event will occur, it will only be disclosed in the notes.	
A contingent liability occurs when the event is possible but not probable.	
A contingent liability occurs when the event is probable.	
If a contingent asset is only possible or remote it should be ignored.	
A contingent asset should be disclosed in the notes at all times.	

Task 5.9

Gym-On-demand Ltd operates a chain of 24-hour gyms. The company's accountant is working on the financial statements for the year ended 31 December 20X5.

On 18 September 20X5, a claim was made against Gym-On-demand Ltd. A customer suffered an injury while using one of the company's gyms. The customer claims that he had received inadequate instructions on the use of weights from the gym's supervisor.

Gym-On-Demand Ltd's solicitor has confirmed that it is highly likely that the customer will win the case. Based upon their experience of similar cases of this nature, they have estimated that damages of approximately £10,000 will have to be paid.

Explain whether the legal claim should be treated as a provision or a contingent liability and how it should be treated in the financial statements.

Task 5.10

Richardson Logistics Ltd

You have been asked to help with the preparation of the financial statements of Richardson Ltd for the year ended 31 March 20X2.

The company's trial balance as at 31 March 20X2 is as follows:

	£000	£000
Trade and Other Receivables	2,716	
Trade and Other Payables		2,564
Prepayments	324	
Cash at bank	224	
Bank loan repayable in 20X6		3,600
Share capital (£1 ordinary shares)		12,960
Retained earnings at 1st April 20X1		2,556
Property, plant and equipment cost	33,448	
Property plant and equipment accumulated depreciation		14,864
Corporation tax		68
Sales		35,016
Sales returns	140	
Purchases	21,156	
Purchases returns		172
Distribution costs	2,952	
Administrative expenses	5,824	
Inventories at 1st April 20X1	3,760	
Interest paid	256	
Dividends paid	1,000	
	71,800	**71,800**

Further information:

- The inventories at the close of business on the 31 March 20X2 cost £3,364,000.
- Storage costs of £200,000 which should be classified as distribution costs have been incorrectly classified as an administrative expense.
- An invoice of £96,000 for repairs and maintenance of vehicles used for transportation purposes for the period 1 February 20X2 to 30 April 20X2 was received on 5th May 20X2. The invoice was not included in the trial balance. Vehicle repairs and maintenance are treated as a distribution cost.
- Trade receivables includes a debt of £42,000 that is to be written off. Irrecoverable debts are classified as an administrative expense.
- The corporation tax balance included in the trial balance of £68,000 was the result of an over estimate of the tax liability for the previous year. The corporation tax charge in respect of the profits for the current year of 31 March 20X2 has been estimated at £440,000.
- Land included in property, plant and equipment at a cost of £9,200,000 was revalued at £11,900,000 on 31 March 20X2. The valuation is to be incorporated into the financial statements for the year ended 31 March 20X2.
- All operations are continuing operations.

a) Draft the statement of profit or loss and other comprehensive income for Richardson Logistics Ltd for the year ended year ended 31 March 20X2.

b) Draft the statement of financial position for Richardson Logistics Ltd year ended 31 March 20X2.

Use the workings boxes to help you.

Richardson Logistics Ltd Statement of Profit or Loss and Other Comprehensive Income for the year ended 31 March 20X2	
	£000
Gross profit	
Operating profit	
Profit before tax	
Profit for the period from continuing operations	
Total comprehensive income for the year	

Workings boxes:

Cost of Sales	£000

Distribution Costs	£000

Administration Expenses	£000

Tax	£000

Richardson Logistics Ltd Statement of Financial Position as at 31 March 20X2	
	£000
ASSETS	
Non-Current Assets	
Current Assets	
TOTAL ASSETS	
EQUITY AND LIABILITIES	
Equity	
Total Equity	
Non-current Liabilities	
Current Liabilities	
Total Liabilities	
TOTAL EQUITY AND LIABILITIES	

Trade and Other Receivables	£000

Trade and Other Payables	£000

Chapter 6: Statement of Cash Flows

Task 6.1

Identify from the following options the purpose of the Statement of Cash Flows.

	✓
Profitability of the business over the period	
Financial strength of the business other the period	
How well the business has managed its cash resources over the period	
How the ownership of the business has changed over the period	

Task 6.2

Identify which of the following statements are true.

	✓
The Statement of Cash Flows is prepared on an accruals basis.	
The Statement of Cash Flows looks at the amount of money actually received and spent by the business.	
The Statement of Cash Flows is prepared on a cash basis.	
The Statement of Cash Flows looks at the amount of money expected to the received and spent by the business.	

Task 6.3

a) Complete the following sentences.

Choose from: goods or services, profit, ordinary course of business, trading profit.

The purpose of the reconciliation is to calculate the ____________ we have made through the __________________________________ from the selling of _______________________. This is also known as ________________ of the business.

b) Identify which of the following are added or deducted in the reconciliation of profit to net cash.

	Add / deduct
Depreciation	
Dividends received	
A gain on the disposal of PPE	
A loss on the disposal of PPE	
An increase in inventory	
A decrease in inventory	
An increase in receivables	
A decrease in receivables	
An increase in payables	
A decrease in payables	

Task 6.4

Identify if the following items are cash inflows or outflows.

	Inflow / outflow
Purchase of non-current assets	
Receipt of dividends	
Issue of new share capital	
Payment of dividends	
Taking out new bank loans	
Disposal of non-current assets	
Repayment of bank loans	

Task 6.5

Identify under which section the following items will appear in the Statement of Cash Flows.

Items	Heading
Purchase of non-current assets	
Receipt of dividends	
Issue of new share capital	
Payment of dividends	
Taking out or repayment new bank loans	
Disposal of non-current assets	

Task 6.6

Apollo Ltd is preparing its Statement of Cash Flows for the year ended 31st December 20X5.

The following balances have been extracted from the Statements of Financial Position as at 31st December 20X3 and 31st December 20X4:

	As at 31st December 20X4	As at 31st December 20X3
Tax Payable	£17,180	£19,300
Finance Costs (Interest) Payable	£3,724	£3,296

The extract from the Statement of Profit or Loss for the year ended 31st December 20X4 shows:

Profit from Operations	**£218,708**
Finance Costs	-£3,724
Profit Before Taxation	**£214,984**
Taxation	-£15,820
Profit from Continuing Operations	**£199,164**

Calculate how much Apollo Ltd have **actually paid** in regard to tax and interest during the year.

	Taxation	Interest
Balance at start of year		
Charge for year (from P&L)		
Balance at end of year		
Amount Paid		

Task 6.7

You have been asked by your manager to prepare the Statement of Cash Flows for Parison Ltd for the year ended 31 December 20X5.

The most recent Statement of Profit or Loss and Other Comprehensive Income and Statement of Financial Position of Parison Ltd are as follows:

Statement of Profit & Loss and Other Comprehensive Income for the year ended 31 December 20X5.	
	£000
Revenue	4,000
Cost of Sales	-2,700
GROSS PROFIT	**1,300**
Dividend received	40
Gain on disposal	20
Distribution Costs	-198
Administrative Expenses	-240
PROFIT FROM OPERATIONS	**922**
Finance Costs	-46
PROFIT BEFORE TAX	**876**
Tax	-250
PROFIT FOR YEAR FROM CONTINUING OPERATIONS	**626**
Other Comprehensive Income	200
TOTAL COMPREHENSIVE INCOME FOR THE YEAR	**826**

Statement of Financial Position for Parison Ltd as at 31 December 20X5		
	31/12/20X5	31/12/20X4
ASSETS	**£000**	**£000**
Non-Current Assets		
Property, Plant and Equipment	2,360	2,020
Current Assets		
Inventories	972	1,010
Trade and Other Receivables	1,890	1,314
Cash and Cash Equivalents	244	20
TOTAL ASSETS	**5,466**	**4,364**
EQUITY AND LIABILITIES		
Equity		
Share Capital	2,400	2,000
Share Premium	630	540
Retained Earnings	766	220
Revaluation	200	
Total Equity	3,996	2,760
Non-current Liabilities		
Bank loans	100	300
Current Liabilities		
Trade and Other Payables	1,120	1,092
Tax Payable	250	212
Total Liabilities	1,470	1,604
TOTAL EQUITY AND LIABILITIES	**5,466**	**4,364**

Further Information:

The depreciation charge for the year was £380,000.

PPE costing £340,000 with accumulated depreciation of £180,000, were sold during the year.

A dividend was paid of £80,000.

Land has been revalued and has increased in value by £200,000.

All sales and purchases were made on credit. All other expenses were paid in cash.

a) Prepare the reconciliation of profit before tax to net cash from operating activities for Parison Ltd for the year ended 31 December 20X5.

b) Prepare the Statement of Cash Flows for Parison Ltd for the year ended 31 December 20X5.

Reconciliation of profit before tax to net cash from operating activities	
	£000
Profit Before Tax	
Adjustments for:	
Depreciation	
Gain on disposal of PPE	
Dividends received	
Finance Costs	
Adjustment in respect of inventories	
Adjustment in respect of trade receivables	
Adjustment in respect of trade payables	
Cash generated by operations	
Tax paid	
Interest paid	
Net cash from operating activities	

Workings box

Tax paid	£000
Balance b/d	
SPL charge	
Balance c/d	
Total	

Parison Ltd – Statement of Cash Flows for the year ended 31 December 20X5	
	£000
Net cash from operating activities	
Investing Activities	
Dividend Received	
Proceeds on Disposal	
Purchases of PPE	
Net cash used in investing activities	
Financing Activities	
Repayment of bank loans	
Proceeds from shares issued	
Dividend paid	
Net cash from financing activities	
Net increase / decrease in cash and cash equivalents	
Cash and cash equivalents at the beginning of the year	
Cash and cash equivalents at the end of the year	

Workings box

Purchases of PPE	£000
PPE at start of year	
Depreciation charge	
Carrying amount of PPE sold	
Revaluation	
PPE at end of year	
Total PPE additions	

Task 6.8

You have been asked by your manager to prepare the Statement of Cash Flows for Rampage Ltd for the year ended 31 December 20X6.

The most recent Statement of Profit or Loss and Other Comprehensive Income and Statement of Financial Position of Rampage Ltd are as follows:

Statement of Profit & Loss and Other Comprehensive Income for the year ended 31 December 20X6.	
	£000
Revenue	6,000
Cost of Sales	-4,050
GROSS PROFIT	**1,950**
Dividend received	60
Gain on disposal	30
Distribution Costs	-297
Administrative Expenses	-360
PROFIT FROM OPERATIONS	**1,383**
Finance Costs	-69
PROFIT BEFORE TAX	**1,314**
Tax	-375
PROFIT FOR YEAR FROM CONTINUING OPERATIONS	**939**
Other Comprehensive Income	300
TOTAL COMPREHENSIVE INCOME FOR THE YEAR	**1,239**

Statement of Financial Position for Rampage Ltd as at 31 December 20X6		
	31/12/20X6	31/12/20X5
ASSETS	**£000**	**£000**
Non-Current Assets		
Property, Plant and Equipment	3,540	3,030
Current Assets		
Inventories	1,458	1,515
Trade and Other Receivables	2,835	1,971
Cash and Cash Equivalents	366	30
TOTAL ASSETS	8,199	6,546
EQUITY AND LIABILITIES		
Equity		
Share Capital	3,600	3,000
Share Premium	945	810
Retained Earnings	1,149	330
Revaluation	300	
Total Equity	5,994	4,140
Non-current Liabilities		
Bank loans	150	450
Current Liabilities		
Trade and Other Payables	1,680	1,638
Tax Payable	375	318
Total Liabilities	2,205	2,406
TOTAL EQUITY AND LIABILITIES	8,199	6,546

Further Information:

The depreciation charge for the year was £570,000.

PPE costing £510,000 with accumulated depreciation of £270,000, were sold during the year.

A dividend was paid of £120,000.

Land has been revalued and has increased in value by £300,000.

All sales and purchases were made on credit. All other expenses were paid in cash.

a) Prepare the reconciliation of profit before tax to net cash from operating activities for Rampage Ltd for the year ended 31 December 20X6.

b) Prepare the Statement of Cash Flows for Rampage Ltd for the year ended 31 December 20X6.

Reconciliation of profit before tax to net cash from operating activities	
	£000
Profit Before Tax	
Adjustments for:	
Depreciation	
Gain on disposal of PPE	
Dividends received	
Finance Costs	
Adjustment in respect of inventories	
Adjustment in respect of trade receivables	
Adjustment in respect of trade payables	
Cash generated by operations	
Tax paid	
Interest paid	
Net cash from operating activities	

Workings box

Tax paid	£000
Balance b/d	
SPL charge	
Balance c/d	
Total	

Rampage Ltd – Statement of Cash Flows for the year ended 31 December 20X6	
	£000
Net cash from operating activities	
Investing Activities	
Dividend Received	
Proceeds on Disposal	
Purchases of PPE	
Net cash used in investing activities	
Financing Activities	
Repayment of bank loans	
Proceeds from shares issued	
Dividend paid	
Net cash from financing activities	
Net increase / decrease in cash and cash equivalents	
Cash and cash equivalents at the beginning of the year	
Cash and cash equivalents at the end of the year	

Workings box

Purchases of PPE	£000
PPE at start of year	
Depreciation charge	
Carrying amount of PPE sold	
Revaluation	
PPE at end of year	
Total PPE additions	

Task 6.9

You have been asked by your manager to prepare the Statement of Cash Flows for Roberts Ltd for the year ended 31 December 20X3.

The most recent Statement of Profit or Loss and Other Comprehensive Income and Statement of Financial Position of Roberts Ltd are as follows:

Statement of Profit & Loss and Other Comprehensive Income for the year ended 31 December 20X3.	
	£000
Revenue	180,826
Cost of Sales	-90,216
GROSS PROFIT	**90,610**
Dividend received	154
Loss on disposal	-58
Distribution Costs	-33,008
Administrative Expenses	-15,160
PROFIT FROM OPERATIONS	**42,538**
Finance Costs	-68
PROFIT BEFORE TAX	**42,470**
Tax	-1,958
PROFIT FOR YEAR FROM CONTINUING OPERATIONS	**40,512**
Other Comprehensive Income	-
TOTAL COMPREHENSIVE INCOME FOR THE YEAR	**40,512**

Statement of Financial Position for Roberts Ltd as at 31 December 20X3		
	31/12/20X3	31/12/20X2
ASSETS	**£000**	**£000**
Non-Current Assets		
Property, Plant and Equipment	95,700	56,944
Investments	16,000	16,000
Current Assets		
Inventories	12,108	11,620
Trade and Other Receivables	9,378	11,928
Cash and Cash Equivalents	1,192	4,952
TOTAL ASSETS	**134,378**	**101,444**
EQUITY AND LIABILITIES		
Equity		
Share Capital	37,000	32,600
Share Premium	7,200	5,600
Retained Earnings	66,956	28,374
Total Equity	**111,156**	**66,574**
Non-current Liabilities		
Bank loans	7,400	10,200
Current Liabilities		
Trade and Other Payables	13,864	22,550
Tax Payable	1,958	2,120
Total Liabilities	**23,222**	**34,870**
TOTAL EQUITY AND LIABILITIES	**134,378**	**101,444**

Further Information:

The depreciation charge for the year was £4,810,000.

PPE with a carrying value of £720,000 was sold during the year.

A dividend of £1,930,000 was paid during the year, and a further dividend of £250,000 was declared on 18th January 20X3 before the financial statements were authorised for issue.

All sales and purchases were made on credit. All other expenses were paid in cash.

a) Prepare the reconciliation of profit before tax to net cash from operating activities for Roberts Ltd for the year ended 31 December 20X3.

b) Prepare the Statement of Cash Flows for Roberts Ltd for the year ended 31 December 20X3.

Reconciliation of profit before tax to net cash from operating activities	
	£000
Profit Before Tax	
Adjustments for:	
Depreciation	
Loss on disposal of PPE	
Dividends received	
Finance Costs	
Adjustment in respect of inventories	
Adjustment in respect of trade receivables	
Adjustment in respect of trade payables	
Cash generated by operations	
Tax paid	
Interest paid	
Net cash from operating activities	

Workings box

Tax paid	£000
Balance b/d	
SPL charge	
Balance c/d	
Total	

Roberts Ltd – Statement of Cash Flows for the year ended 31 December 20X3	
	£000
Net cash from operating activities	
Investing Activities	
Dividend Received	
Proceeds on Disposal	
Purchases of PPE	
Net cash used in investing activities	
Financing Activities	
Repayment of bank loans	
Proceeds from shares issued	
Dividend paid	
Net cash from financing activities	
Net increase / decrease in cash and cash equivalents	
Cash and cash equivalents at the beginning of the year	
Cash and cash equivalents at the end of the year	

Workings box

Purchases of PPE	£000
PPE at start of year	
Depreciation charge	
Carrying amount of PPE sold	
Revaluation	
PPE at end of year	
Total PPE additions	

c) Prepare the Statement of Change in Equity for Roberts Ltd for the year ended 31 December 20X3.

	Share Capital	Share Premium	Revaluation Reserve	Retained Earnings	Total Equity
	£000	£000	£000	£000	£000
Balance at start of year					
Changes in Equity:					
Comprehensive Income					
Dividends					
Issue of Share Capital					
Balance at end of year					

Task 6.10

You have been asked by your manager to prepare the Statement of Cash Flows for Mercia Ltd for the year ended 31 December 20X3.

The most recent Statement of Profit or Loss and Other Comprehensive Income and Statement of Financial Position of Mercia Ltd are as follows:

Statement of Profit & Loss and Other Comprehensive Income for the year ended 31 December 20X3.	
	£000
Revenue	8,000
Cost of Sales	-5,400
GROSS PROFIT	**2,600**
Dividend received	80
Gain on disposal	40
Distribution Costs	-396
Administrative Expenses	-480
PROFIT FROM OPERATIONS	**1,844**
Finance Costs	-92
PROFIT BEFORE TAX	**1,752**
Tax	-500
PROFIT FOR YEAR FROM CONTINUING OPERATIONS	**1,252**
Other Comprehensive Income	100
TOTAL COMPREHENSIVE INCOME FOR THE YEAR	**1,352**

Statement of Financial Position for Mercia Ltd as at 31 December 20X3		
	31/12/20X3	31/12/20X2
ASSETS	**£000**	**£000**
Non-Current Assets		
Property, Plant and Equipment	4,720	4,040
Current Assets		
Inventories	1,944	2,020
Trade and Other Receivables	3,780	2,628
Cash and Cash Equivalents	488	40
TOTAL ASSETS	**10,932**	**8,728**
EQUITY AND LIABILITIES		
Equity		
Share Capital	4,800	4,000
Share Premium	1,260	1,080
Retained Earnings	1,532	440
Revaluation	400	
Total Equity	7,992	5,520
Non-current Liabilities		
Bank loans	200	600
Current Liabilities		
Trade and Other Payables	2,240	2,184
Tax Payable	500	424
Total Liabilities	2,940	3,208
TOTAL EQUITY AND LIABILITIES	**10,932**	**8,728**

Further Information:

The depreciation charge for the year was £760,000.

PPE costing £680,000 with accumulated depreciation of £360,000, were sold during the year.

A dividend of £160,000 was paid during the year.

Land has been revalued and has increased by £400,000.

All sales and purchases were made on credit. All other expenses were paid in cash.

a) Prepare the reconciliation of profit before tax to net cash from operating activities for Mercia Ltd for the year ended 31 December 20X3.

b) Prepare the Statement of Cash Flows for Mercia Ltd for the year ended 31 December 20X3.

Reconciliation of profit before tax to net cash from operating activities	
	£000
Profit Before Tax	
Adjustments for:	
Cash generated by operations	
Net cash from operating activities	

Mercia Ltd – Statement of Cash Flows for the year ended 31 December 20X3	
	£000
Net cash from operating activities	
Investing Activities	
Net cash used in investing activities	
Financing Activities	
Net cash from financing activities	
Net increase / decrease in cash and cash equivalents	
Cash and cash equivalents at the beginning of the year	
Cash and cash equivalents at the end of the year	

c) Prepare the Statement of Change in Equity for Mercia Ltd for the year ended 31 December 20X3.

	Share Capital	Share Premium	Revaluation Reserve	Retained Earnings	Total Equity
	£000	£000	£000	£000	£000
Balance at start of year					
Changes in Equity:					
Comprehensive Income					
Dividends					
Issue of Share Capital					
Balance at end of year					

This page is left intentionally blank.

Chapter 7: Consolidated Accounts

Task 7.1

a) Identify which of the following statements are true.

	✓
Each individual company within a group must prepare individual financial statements.	
Consolidated financial statements need only be prepared when the parent company owns more than 75% of the subsidiary.	
Any intra-group transactions should be eliminated from the consolidated financial statements.	
When the parent has bought from, or sold to, a subsidiary, any unrealised profit on goods held in inventory at the year-end must be eliminated.	

b) Hannibal Ltd acquired 60% of the equity share capital of Clarice Ltd.

At the year end Hannibal Ltd has trade receivables of £120,000 and Clarice Ltd has trade receivables of £80,000. The trade receivables of Clarice Ltd includes an amount of £15,000 which is due from Hannibal Ltd.

Calculate the figure will be included for trade receivables in the consolidated Statement of Financial Position?

Task 7.2

On the 1 January Walter Ltd purchased 75% of Jesse Ltd for £800,000.

At the date of acquisition, the retained earnings of Jesse Ltd were £360,000 and the share capital was £400,000.

During the year there was an impairment loss of goodwill, estimated at £10,000.

a) Calculate the net assets acquired.

Net Assets	£000
Share capital	
Retained earnings	
Total	

b) Calculate the goodwill.

Goodwill	£000
Consideration	
NCI at acquisition	
Net assets acquired	
Impairment	
Goodwill	

Task 7.3

Elwood Ltd acquired 100% of the share capital of Jake Ltd on the 1st September, four years ago. The cost of sales of Elwood Ltd together with Jake Ltd for the purpose of the consolidated statements, before taking into account any adjustments, is £420,000.

During the year Elwood Ltd sold goods which had cost £50,000 to Jake Ltd for £65,000. 60% of the goods still remain in the inventories at the end of the year.

Calculate the consolidated cost of sales to go in the consolidated Statement of Profit or Loss, after the necessary adjustments have been made?

	£
Consolidated cost of sales	
Less intra-company transactions	
Unrealised profits	
Total	

Task 7.4

Harry Ltd acquired 80% of the share capital of Lloyd Ltd on the 1 September 20X8. The consideration paid was £4,940,000.

At the date of acquisition Lloyd Ltd had share capital of £2,300,000, a share premium of £250,000 and retained earnings of £1,200,000.

Here are extracts of the Statement of Financial Position for both of the companies on 31 August 20X9:

Statement of Financial Position Extract	Harry	Lloyd
	£000	**£000**
Assets		
Investment	4,940	
Non-currents Assets	10,312	3,115
Current Assets:		
Inventories	2,132	417
Trade and other receivables	6,668	1,780
Cash and cash equivalents	1,150	600
Total Assets	**50,403**	**11,824**
Equity and Liabilities		
Equity		
Share Capital	6,000	2,300
Share Premium	2,000	250
Retained Earnings	11,292	1,800
Total Equity	**38,583**	**8,700**
Non-current liabilities	600	100
Current liabilities:		
Trade payables	3,210	1,052
Tax liability	2,100	410
Total Liabilities	**11,820**	**3,124**
Total equity and liabilities	**50,403**	**11,824**

Additional Information:

On the date of acquisition, land belonging to Lloyd Ltd was revalued. The fair value of the land had increased by £200,000. This has not yet been recorded in the accounts of Lloyd Ltd.

Included in the trade receivables of Harry Ltd and the trade payables of Lloyd Ltd is an inter-company transaction of £20,000.

It has been agreed that goodwill has been impaired by 10%.

Prepare the consolidated statement of financial position for the group for the year ended 31 August 20X9.

Net Assets	£000
Subsidiary's Share Capital	
Subsidiary's Retained earnings	
Adjustment to fair value	
Net Assets	

Goodwill	£000
Consideration (amount paid for the company)	
NCI's share of net assets at acquisition	
Less – Value of **net assets** (working box above)	
Goodwill	
Less – Any impairments	
New Goodwill	

Retained Earnings	£000
100% Parents Retained Earnings	
% of Retained earnings attributable to the parent – post acquisition	
Less – Any impairments	
Retained Earnings	

Non-controlling Interest	£000
% of Share Capital attributable to NCI	
% of Share Premium attributable to NCI	
% of Retained Earnings attributable to NCI	
% of Revaluation attributable to NCI	
NCI	

Harry Group Consolidated Statement of Financial Position		
	£000	***Workings***
Assets:		
Goodwill		
Non-currents Assets		
Current Assets:		
Inventories		
Trade and other receivables		
Cash and cash equivalents		
Total Assets		
Equity and Liabilities:		
Equity:		
Share Capital		
Share Premium		
Retained Earnings		
NCI		
Total Equity		
Non-current liabilities		
Current liabilities:		
Trade payables		
Tax liability		
Total Liabilities		
Total equity and liabilities		

Task 7.5

Jules Ltd acquired 70% of the share capital of Vincent Ltd on 1January 20X6. The consideration paid was £10,750,000.

At the date of acquisition Vincent Ltd had share capital of £4,000,000, a share premium of £300,000 and retained earnings of £1,230,000.

Here are extracts of the Statement of Financial Position for both of the companies on 31 December 20X6:

Statement of Financial Position Extract	Jules	Vincent
	£000	**£000**
Assets		
Investment	10,750	
Non-currents Assets	24,312	4,115
Current Assets:		
Inventories	4,132	617
Trade and other receivables	7,113	3,260
Cash and cash equivalents	2,700	1,160
Total Assets	**49,007**	**9,152**
Equity and Liabilities		
Equity		
Share Capital	10,000	4,000
Share Premium	4,000	300
Retained Earnings	24,377	1,607
Total Equity	**38,377**	**5,907**
Non-current liabilities	1,400	310
Current liabilities:		
Trade payables	6,430	2,335
Tax liability	2,800	600
Total Liabilities	**10,630**	**3,245**
Total equity and liabilities	**49,007**	**9,152**

Additional Information:

On the date of acquisition, land belonging to Vincent Ltd was revalued. The fair value of the land had increased by £1,000,000. This has not yet been recorded in the accounts of Vincent Ltd.

During the year Vincent Ltd sold goods for £200,000 to Jules plc at a profit margin of 40%.

Half of the goods remain in Jules plc's inventory at the end of the year.

It has been agreed that goodwill has been impaired by £130,000.

Prepare the consolidated statement of financial position for the group for the year ended 31st December 20X6. Enter whole numbers only.

Net Assets	£000
Subsidiary's Share Capital	
Subsidiary's Retained earnings	
Adjustment to fair value	
Net Assets	

Goodwill	£000
Consideration	
NCI's share of net assets at acquisition	
Less – Value of **net assets**	
Goodwill	
Less – Any impairments	
New Goodwill	

Retained Earnings	£000
100% Parents Retained Earnings	
% of Retained earnings attributable to the parent – post acquisition	
Less – Any impairments	
Retained Earnings	

Non-controlling Interest	£000
% of Share Capital attributable to NCI	
% of Share Premium attributable to NCI	
% of Retained Earnings attributable to NCI	
% of Revaluation attributable to NCI	
NCI	

Jules Group Consolidated Statement of Financial Position		
	£000	***Workings***
Assets:		
Goodwill		
Non-currents Assets		
Current Assets:		
Inventories		
Trade and other receivables		
Cash and cash equivalents		
Total Assets		
Equity and Liabilities:		
Equity:		
Share Capital		
Share Premium		
Retained Earnings		
NCI		
Total Equity		
Non-current liabilities		
Current liabilities:		
Trade payables		
Tax liability		
Total Liabilities		
Total equity and liabilities		

Task 7.6

Doc Ltd acquired 80% of the share capital of Marty Ltd on 1 January 20X3. The consideration paid was £12,000,000.

At the date of acquisition Marty Ltd had share capital of £10,000,000 and retained earnings of £860,000.

Here are extracts of the Statement of Financial Position for both of the companies on 31 December 20X3:

Statement of Financial Position Extract	Doc	Marty
	£000	**£000**
Assets		
Investment	13,000	
Non-currents Assets	21,600	5,740
Current Assets:		
Inventories	7,772	2,260
Trade and other receivables	13,528	5,140
Cash and cash equivalents	3,380	1,300
Total Assets	**59,280**	**14,240**
Equity and Liabilities		
Equity		
Share Capital	36,000	10,000
Retained Earnings	11,626	1,360
Total Equity	47,626	11,360
Non-current liabilities	4,400	1,200
Current liabilities:		
Trade payables	5,894	1,640
Tax liability	1,360	240
Total Liabilities	11,654	2,880
Total equity and liabilities	**59,280**	**14,240**

Additional Information:

Included in the Investment of Doc plc and the non-current liabilities of Marty Ltd is an inter-company loan of £1,000,000 that Doc plc gave to Marty Ltd a few months after acquisition.

On the date of acquisition, land belonging to Marty Ltd was revalued. The fair value of the land had increased by £400,000. This has not yet been recorded in the accounts of Marty Ltd.

It has been agreed that goodwill has been impaired by £40,000.

During the year Doc plc sold £800,000 of goods to Marty Ltd at a cost of £400,000. One quarter of the goods remain in Marty Ltd's inventory at the end of the year.

Prepare the consolidated statement of financial position for the group for the year ended 31st December 20X3.

Net Assets	£000
Subsidiary's Share Capital	
Subsidiary's Retained earnings	
Adjustment to fair value	
Net Assets	

Goodwill	£000
Consideration	
NCI's share of net assets at acquisition	
Less – Value of **net assets**	
Goodwill	
Less – Any impairments	
New Goodwill	

Retained Earnings	£000
100% Parents Retained Earnings	
% of Retained earnings attributable to the parent – post acquisition	
Less – Any impairments	
Retained Earnings	

Non-controlling Interest	£000
% of Share Capital attributable to NCI	
% of Retained Earnings attributable to NCI	
% of Revaluation attributable to NCI	
NCI	

Doc Group Consolidated Statement of Financial Position		
	£000	***Workings***
Assets:		
Goodwill		
Non-currents Assets		
Current Assets:		
Inventories		
Trade and other receivables		
Cash and cash equivalents		
Total Assets		
Equity and Liabilities:		
Equity:		
Share Capital		
Retained Earnings		
NCI		
Total Equity		
Non-current liabilities		
Current liabilities:		
Trade payables		
Tax liability		
Total Liabilities		
Total equity and liabilities		

Task 7.7

Andy Ltd acquired 80% of Red Ltd on 1 September 20X7.

Here are extracts of Andy Ltd and Red Ltd Statements of Profit or Loss for the year ended the 31 August 20X8.

Statement of Profit or Loss Extract	Andy Ltd	Red Ltd
	£	£
Revenue	460,000	205,200
Cost of Sales	-179,120	-96,800
Gross Profit	**280,880**	**108,400**
Other income (dividend from Red)	8,000	0
Operating Expenses	-150,000	-53,600
Profit before tax	**138,880**	**54,800**
Tax	-33,288	-10,520
Profit for the period from continuing operations	**105,592**	**44,280**

Prepare the consolidated Statement of Profit or Loss for the group for the year ended 31st August 20X8.

Consolidated Statement of Profit or Loss	£	*Workings*
Revenue		
Cost of Sales		
Gross Profit		
Other income		
Operating expenses		
Profit before tax		
Tax		
Profit for the period from continuing operations		
Attributable to:		
Equity holders of the parent		
Non-controlling interests		

Revenue	£
Andy	
Red	
Total	

COS	£
Andy	
Red	
Total	

Task 7.8

Solo Ltd acquired 80% of Skywalker Ltd on 1 April 20X7.

Here are extracts of Solo Ltd and Skywalker Ltd Statements of Profit or Loss for the year ended the 31 March 20X8.

Statement of Profit or Loss Extract	Solo Ltd	Skywalker Ltd
	£000	**£000**
Revenue	197,260	89,200
Cost of Sales	-97,740	-24,600
Gross Profit	**99,520**	**64,600**
Other income (dividend from Skywalker)	16,000	0
Operating Expenses	-12,800	-5,600
Profit before tax	**102,720**	**59,000**

Additional information:

In March 20X8 Skywalker Ltd sold goods, which had cost £360,000, to Solo Ltd for £560,000. One half of the goods remain in inventory.

Prepare the consolidated Statement of Profit or Loss for the group for the year ended 31st March 20X8.

Consolidated Statement of Profit or Loss	£000
Revenue	
Cost of Sales	
Gross Profit	
Other income	
Operating expenses	
Profit before tax	

Revenue	£000
Consolidated revenue prior to adjustments	
Consolidation adjustment	
Total	

Cost of Sales	£000
Consolidated COS prior to adjustments	
Consolidation adjustment	
Total	

Task 7.9

Mathilda Ltd acquired 90% of Leon Ltd on 1 September 20X2.

Here are extracts of Mathilda Ltd and Leon Ltd Statements of Profit or Loss for the end ended the 31 August 20X3.

Statement of Profit or Loss Extract	Mathilda Ltd	Leon Ltd
	£000	**£000**
Revenue	21,000	12,000
Cost of Sales	-14,100	-7,175
Gross Profit	**6,900**	**4,825**
Other income (dividend from Leon)	1,750	-
Operating Expenses	-2,724	-2,425
Profit before tax	**11,853**	**2,400**
Tax	-1,135	-410
Profit for the period from continuing operations	**4,791**	**1,990**

Additional information:

In August 20X3 Leon Ltd sold goods, which had cost £250,000, to Mathilda Ltd for £300,000. All of the goods still remain in the inventory of Mathilda Ltd at the year end.

Prepare the consolidated Statement of Profit or Loss for the group for the year ended 31st August 20X3.

Consolidated Statement of Profit or Loss	£000
Revenue	
Cost of Sales	
Gross Profit	
Other income	
Operating expenses	
Profit before tax	
Tax	
Profit for the period from continuing operations	
Attributable to:	
Equity holders of the parent	
Non-controlling interests	

Revenue	£000
Consolidated revenue prior to adjustments	
Consolidation adjustment	
Total	

Cost of Sales	£000
Consolidated COS prior to adjustments	
Consolidation adjustment	
Total	

Task 7.10

Eleven Ltd acquired 80% of Hopper Ltd on 1 January 20X2.

Here are extracts of Eleven Ltd and Hopper Ltd Statements of Profit or Loss for the end ended the 31 December 20X3.

Statement of Profit or Loss Extract	Eleven Ltd	Hopper Ltd
	£000	**£000**
Revenue	12,600	6,300
Cost of Sales	-5,400	-2,700
Gross Profit	**7,200**	**3,600**
Other income (dividend from Hopper)	2,100	0
Operating Expenses	-6,900	-2,010
Profit before tax	**2,400**	**1,590**
Tax	-360	-180
Profit for the period from continuing operations	**2,040**	**1,410**

Additional information:

Towards the end of the year Hopper Ltd sold goods, which had cost £240,000, to Eleven Ltd for £360,000. One half of the goods still remain in the inventory of Eleven Ltd at the year end.

Goodwill has been valued at £200,000. This is amortised annually at 10%. This is to be included in the operating expenses of the group.

Prepare the consolidated Statement of Profit or Loss for the group for the year ended 31st December 20X3.

Consolidated Statement of Profit or Loss	£000
Revenue	
Cost of Sales	
Gross Profit	
Other income	
Operating expenses	
Profit before tax	
Tax	
Profit for the period from continuing operations	
Attributable to:	
Equity holders of the parent	
Non-controlling interests	

Revenue	£000
Consolidated revenue prior to adjustments	
Consolidation adjustment	
Total	

Cost of Sales	£000
Consolidated COS prior to adjustments	
Consolidation adjustment	
Total	

Goodwill	£000
Consolidated operating expenses prior to adjustments	
Consolidation adjustment	
Total	

Chapter 8: Financial Ratios

Task 8.1

State the correct formulas for the following ratios.

Ratio	Formula
Return on capital employed	
Trade payables collection period (days)	
Asset turnover (non- current assets)	
Trade receivables collection period (days)	
Inventory holding period (days)	
Working capital cycle	

Task 8.2

Irving Ltd has revenue for the year ended 31st December 20X3 of £1,540,000.

Its cost of sales for the same period was £635,000 and other operating expenses were £742,000. The total equity of the business was £3,400,000 and non-current liabilities were £288,000.

Calculate the following to two decimal places.

	%
Gross Profit Percentage	
Operating Profit Percentage	
Return on Capital Employed	

Task 8.3

Forge Ltd has revenue for the year ended 31st March 20X5 of £1,250,000.

The cost of sales for the same period was £698,000 and other operating expenses were £312,000. The total equity of the business was £1,550,000, non-current liabilities were £685,000 and inventories were valued at £85,300

Calculate the following to two decimal places.

Gross Profit Percentage		%
Operating Profit Percentage		%
Gearing		%
Inventory turnover		times

Task 8.4

The most recent statement of profit and loss and other comprehensive income and statement of financial position of TJ Engineering Ltd are as follows:

Statement of Profit & Loss and Other Comprehensive Income for the year ended 31 December 20X4	
	£000
Revenue	22,603
Cost of Sales	-11,277
Gross Profit	**11,326**
Distribution Costs	-4,126
Administrative Expenses	-1,895
Profit from Operations	-5,305
Finance Costs	-105
Profit Before Taxation	**5,155**
Taxation	-245
Profit from Continuing Operations	**4,910**

Statement of Financial Position For TJ Engineering Ltd as at 31 December 20X4	
Assets	**£000**
Non-Current Assets	
Property Plant and Equipment	11,368
Current Assets	
Inventories	1,453
Trade Receivables	1,491
Cash and Cash Equivalents	619
	3,563
Total assets	**14,931**
Equity and Liabilities	
Equity	
Share Capital	4,775
Retained Earnings	3,547
Total Equity	8,322
Non-Current Liabilities	
Bank Loans	3,525
Current Liabilities	
Trade Payables	2,819
Tax Liabilities	265
Total Liabilities	6,609
Total equity and liabilities	**14,931**

a) State the correct formulae for the following ratios.

Ratio	Formula
Current ratio	
Quick ratio / Acid test	
Inventory holding period (days)	
Gearing ratio	
Return on shareholder funds	
Inventory turnover	

b) Calculate the following ratios to TWO decimal places.

Current ratio		:1
Quick ratio / Acid test		:1
Inventory holding period (days)		days
Gearing ratio		%
Return on shareholder funds		%
Inventory turnover		times

Task 8.5

The most recent statement of profit and loss and other comprehensive income and statement of financial position of Irongate Industries Ltd are as follows:

Statement of Profit & Loss and Other Comprehensive Income for the year ended 31 December 20X4	
	£000
Revenue	32,500
Cost of Sales	-20,100
Gross Profit	**12,400**
Distribution Costs	-3,257
Administrative Expenses	-3,359
Profit from Operations	**5,784**
Finance Costs	-450
Profit Before Taxation	**5,334**
Taxation	-520
Profit from Continuing Operations	**4,814**
Other comprehensive Income	0
Total Comprehensive	**4,814**

Statement of Financial Position For Irongate Industries Ltd as at 31 December 20X4	
Assets	**£000**
Non-Current Assets	
Property Plant and Equipment	22,625
Current Assets	
Inventories	3,939
Trade Receivables	3,098
Cash and Cash Equivalents	5,280
	12,317
Total assets	**34,942**
Equity and Liabilities	
Equity	
Share Capital	15,000
Retained Earnings	6,914
Total Equity	21,914
Non-Current Liabilities	
Bank Loans	9,000
Current Liabilities	
Trade Payables	3,543
Tax Liabilities	485
Total Liabilities	13,028
Total equity and liabilities	**34,942**

a) State the correct formulae for the following ratios.

Ratio	Formula
Return on capital employed	
Inventory holding period (days)	
Trade receivables collection period (days)	
Trade payables collection period (days)	
Working capital cycle	
Asset turnover (non- current assets)	

b) Calculate the following ratios to TWO decimal places.

Return on capital employed		%
Inventory holding period (days)		days
Trade receivables collection period (days)		days
Trade payables collection period (days)		days
Working capital cycle		days
Asset turnover (non- current assets)		times

Task 8.6

JCD Ltd manufacture machinery used in the construction industry.

You have been asked to use the extract of the financial statements of the company's main competitor and compare the results.

Extract of competitor financial statements	30/09/20X5
	£000
Sales revenue	38,000
Cost of sales	(13,980)
Profit from operations	4,800
Assets	
Non-current assets	42,750
Inventories	4,055
Trade receivables	4,545
Total	**51,350**
Equity and liabilities	
Equity	28,800
Non-current liabilities	18,500
Trade payables	3,200
Tax liabilities	850
Total	**51,350**

a) Complete the missing ratios in the scorecard to one decimal place where appropriate.

Scorecard for year ending the 30/09/20X5	JCD Ltd	Competitor
Gross profit %	62.7%	
Operating profit %	17.8%	
ROCE	12.9%	
Current ratio	2.2:1	
Acid test	1.3:1	
Inventory holding days	89 days	
Trade receivables	42 days	
Trade payables payment period	74 days	83 days
Working capital cycle	57 days	

b) Based on the scorecard above, select the correct assumptions for the following.

Profitability	
The gross profit and operating profit percentages are better for the competitor, this indicates that the competitor has a better use of working capital.	
The ROCE of the competitor, in comparison to JCD Ltd, indicates that the competitor is using its working capital more efficiently.	
The overall profitability of JCD Ltd is better than the competitor. Although the gross profit percentage is slightly higher for the competitor, JCD Ltd may have lower operating costs and uses its working capital more efficiently.	

Liquidity	
The liquidity of the competitor is better. This indicates that company has a good short-term solvency.	
The liquidity of JCD Ltd is better. The current ratio indicates that the company has enough current assets to cover its current liabilities. The quick ratio / acid test is a better test of liquidity as it shows the immediate solvency of a company because inventories are less liquid.	
The current ratio of both companies is a cause for concern and should be below 1:1, which is also the industry average.	

Working capital cycle	
The working capital cycle for the competitor is considerably better than JCD Ltd. This could be due the better inventory holding days.	
The working capital cycle for JCD Ltd is better than the competitor. This indicates that the amount of time between paying for materials and receiving the cash for the sold goods is quicker than that of the competitor. This could be due to the better inventory holding period.	
The competitor has a better working capital cycle of 21 days. This indicates that the competitor making better use of its resources and has a better turnaround of inventory.	

Overall performance	
The overall performance of the competitor is better than JCD Ltd. This indicates that JCD Ltd should reduce its selling prices to gain more customers.	
The overall performance of the competitor is significantly worse than JCD Ltd. The current ratios show serious cause for concern and liquidity issues.	
The overall performance of the competitor is slightly worse than JCD Ltd. Whilst this is good, there are limitations on the accuracy of the ratios as we can only assume what has affected these. JCD Ltd should still attempt to improve its ratios and complete another comparison/review in the near future to identify any significant changes.	

Task 8.7

Consider the following ratios and state whether the position has got better or worse from the previous year.

Ratio	20X4	20X3	Better	Worse
Inventory holding days	56 days	45 days		
Current ratio	2.3:1	2:1		
Gearing	45%	52%		
Trade receivable days	42 days	36 days		
Interest cover	3 times	2.5 times		
ROCE	24.7%	32.2%		

Task 8.8

Your manager has asked you to review the performance and efficiency of Virtuoso Technologies Ltd using the following ratios:

Virtuoso Technologies Ltd	20X3	20X2
Gross profit percentage	20%	25%
Operating profit percentage	11.8%	9.8%
Trade receivables collection period	64 days	55 days
Inventory holding period	88 days	62 days

a) For each of the following ratios:

i) Identify whether the ratio in 20X3 is better or worse in comparison to 20X2.

ii) Explain what the ratios tell you about the performance and efficiency of the company.

Gross Profit Margin

	✓
Better	
Worse	

Comments

Operating Profit Margin

	✓
Better	
Worse	

Comments

Trade Receivables Collection Period

	✓
Better	
Worse	

Comments

Inventory Holding Period

	✓
Better	
Worse	

Comments

b) Make <u>one</u> recommendation on how to improve each of the ratios given.

Improvements

Gross Profit Margin

Operating Profit Margin

Trade Receivables Period

Inventory Holding Period

Task 8.9

The board of Simulation Tech Ltd has asked you to review the profitability and risk of the business. You have been provided the following ratios:

Simulation Tech Ltd	20X4	20X3
Gross profit percentage	24%	18%
Operating profit percentage	6.4%	14.4%
ROCE	15%	21%
Gearing	38.7%	26.2%
Interest cover	2.6 times	5.1 times

a) For each of the following ratios:

i) Identify whether the ratio in 20X4 is better or worse in comparison to 20X3.

ii) Explain what the ratios tell you about the performance and efficiency of the company.

Gross Profit Margin

	✓
Better	
Worse	

Comments

Operating Profit Margin

	✓
Better	
Worse	

Comments

Return on Capital Employed

	✓
Better	
Worse	

Comments

Gearing

	✓
Better	
Worse	

Comments

Interest Cover

	✓
Better	
Worse	

Comments

b) What advice would you give to the board of the company.

Task 8.10

Your manager has asked you to review the working capital management of Imagine Products Ltd using the following information:

Imagine Products Ltd	20X7	20X6
Inventory holding period	38 days	42 days
Trade receivables collection period	46 days	54 days
Trade payables payment period	51 days	44 days
Working Capital Cycle	30 days	46 days

a) For each of the following ratios:

i) Identify whether the ratio in 20X7 is better or worse in comparison to 20X6.

ii) Explain what the ratios tell you about the performance and efficiency of the company.

iii) What may have caused the change in performance? Give one reason.

Inventory Holding Period

	✓
Better	
Worse	

Comments

Trade Receivables Collection Period

	✓
Better	
Worse	

Comments

Trade Payables Payment Period

	✓
Better	
Worse	

Comments

Working Capital Cycle

	✓
Better	
Worse	

Comments

c) Explain why using historical data may not always be a reliable basis for predicting financial performance.

Mock Exam

Assessment information:

You have **2 hours and 30 minutes** to complete this practice assessment.

- This assessment contains 7 tasks and you should attempt to complete all elements of each task.
- There are a total of **120 marks available** in the assessment.
- You must use a full stop to indicate a decimal place where required. For example, write 500.75 not 500,75, 50075, or 500 75.
- You may use a comma as a thousand separator but both 100,000 or 100000 are acceptable.
- Read every task carefully to ensure you understand what is required.

Task 1 (23 marks)

You have been asked to help prepare the financial statements of Ascot Ltd for the year ended 31 March 20X9. The company's trial balance as at 31 March 20X9 is shown below.

Ascot Ltd

Trial balance as at 31 March 20X9

	Debit	Credit
	£000	£000
Share capital		14,000
Trade and other payables		2,642
Property, plant and equipment – cost	55,360	
Property, plant and equipment – acc depreciation		28,980
Trade and other receivables	4,567	
Accruals		239
6% bank loan repayable 20Y3		12,000
Cash at bank	3,519	
Retained earnings		6,590
Interest	360	
Sales		65,677
Purchases	48,900	
Returns inwards	564	
Returns outwards		766
Distribution costs	4,555	
Administrative expenses	6,589	
Inventories as at 1 April 20X8	5,640	
Interim dividend for year ended 31 March 20X9	840	
	130,894	**130,894**

Further information

a) The share capital of the company consists of ordinary shares with a nominal value of £1.

b) The inventories at the close of business on 31 March 20X9 were valued at £6,806,000.

c) The company hired some management consultants for the period 1 March to 31 May 20X9. The contract price for the three months was £144,000 and this was paid in full on 8 March. This is to treated as an administrative expense in the financial statements.

d) The company bought some radio advertising for a period of three months from 1 February to 30 April 20X9. The invoice for the full three months of £180,000 was paid on 10 April. No entry has been made in the accounts for this transaction. Advertising is to be treated as a distribution cost in the financial statements.

e) Interest on the bank loan for the last six months of the year has not been included in the accounts in the trial balance.

f) The corporation tax charge for the year has been calculated as £2,540,000.

g) Land was revalued during the year by an additional £3,000,000. No adjustments have been made for this revaluation.

h) A final dividend of £690,000 was declared on 5th May 20X9.

i) All of the operations are continuing operations.

a) Draft the statement of profit or loss and other comprehensive income for Ascot Ltd for the year ended 31st March 20X9.

Use the working boxes to help you.

Workings boxes:

Cost of Sales	£000
Total	

Distribution Costs	£000
Total	

Administrative Expenses	£000
Total	

Ascot Ltd Statement of Profit or Loss and Other Comprehensive Income for the year ended 31st March 20X9	
	£000
Revenue	
Cost of Sales	
Gross Profit	
Distribution Costs	
Administration Expenses	
Profit from Operations	
Finance Costs	
Profit Before Tax	
Taxation	
Profit for the Year from Continuing Operations	
Other Comprehensive Income for the Year	
Total Comprehensive Income for the Year	

c) Draft the Statement of Financial Position for Ascot Ltd as at 31st March 20X9.

ASSETS	£000
Non-Current Assets	
Property Plant and Equipment	
Current Assets	
Inventories	
Trade and Other Receivables	
Cash and Cash Equivalents	
Total Assets	
EQUITY AND LIABILITIES	
Equity	
Share Capital	
Retained Earnings	
Revaluation Reserve	
Total Equity	
Non-Current Liabilities	
Bank Loans	
Current Liabilities	
Trade and Other Payables	
Tax Liability	
Total Liabilities	
Total Equity and Liabilities	

Working boxes:

Property, Plant and Equipment	
	£000
Total	

Trade and Other Receivables	
	£000
Total	

Trade and Other Payables	
	£000
Total	

Retained Earnings	
	£000
Total	

b) Draft the Statement of Changes in Equity for Ascot Ltd for the year ended 31st March 20X9.

	Share Capital	Revaluation	Retained Earnings	Total Equity
	£000	£000	£000	£000
Balance at 1st April 20X8				
Changes in Equity				
Total Comprehensive Income				
Dividends				
Balance at 31st March 20X9				

Task 2 (17 marks)

You have been asked to prepare the Statement of Cash Flows for Garibaldi Ltd for the year ended 31st December 20X9.

The most recent Statement of Profit or Loss and Statement of Financial Position (with comparatives for the previous year) of Garibaldi Ltd are shown below.

Garibaldi Ltd – Statement of Profit or Loss for the year ended 31/12/20X9	
	£000
Revenue	203,685
Cost of Sales	-102,992
Gross Profit	**100,693**
Loss on Disposal of PPE	-40
Dividends Received	154
Distribution Costs	-21,541
Administrative Expenses	-17,993
Profit from Operations	**61,273**
Finance Costs	-2,106
Profit Before Taxation	**59,167**
Taxation	-9,985
Profit from Continuing Operations	**49,182**

Additional Information:

- The total depreciation charge for the year was £14,390,000.
- PPE with a carrying value of £823,000 was sold during the year.
- All sales and purchases were made on credit. All expenses were paid for in cash.
- An investment of £10,500,000 in the shares of another company was made during the year; this was paid for in cash.
- A dividend of £1,800,000 was paid during the year, and a further dividend of £1,400,000 was declared on 20th January 20Y0, before the financial statements were authorised for issue.

Garibaldi Ltd – Statement of Financial Position as at…		
	31/12/20X9 £000	31/12/20X8 £000
ASSETS		
Non-Current Assets		
Property Plant and Equipment	208,950	140,950
Investments at cost	10,500	-
	219,450	140,950
Current Assets		
Inventories	6,956	8,169
Trade Receivables	22,369	24,108
Cash and Cash Equivalents	-	6,390
	29,325	38,667
TOTAL ASSETS	248,775	179,617
EQUITY AND LIABILITIES		
Equity		
Share Capital	25,000	22,500
Share Premium	6,145	5,750
Retained Earnings	155,831	108,449
Total Equity	186,976	136,699
Non-Current Liabilities		
Bank Loans	22,000	19,600
	22,000	19,600
Current Liabilities		
Trade Payables	15,846	14,456
Tax Liabilities	9,985	8,862
Bank Overdraft	13,968	-
	39,799	23,318
Total Liabilities	61,799	42,918
TOTAL EQUITY AND LIABILITIES	248,775	179,617

a) Complete the following workings boxes to calculate the correct figures for Proceeds on Disposal of PPE and Purchases of PPE.

Proceeds on Disposal of PPE	
	£000
Carrying amount of PPE sold	
Gain / Loss on disposal of PPE	

Purchases of PPE	
	£000
PPE at start of year	
Depreciation Charge	
Carrying amount of PPE sold	
PPE at end of year	
Total PPE additions	

b) Prepare a reconciliation of profit before tax to net cash from operating activities for Garibaldi Ltd for the year ended 31st December 20X9.

	£000
Profit before tax	
Adjustments For:	
Depreciation	
Gain / Loss on disposal of PPE	
Dividends received	
Finance Costs	
Adjustment in respect of inventories	
Adjustment in respect of trade receivables	
Adjustment in respect of trade payables	
Cash Generated by Operations	
Interest Paid	
Taxation Paid	
Net Cash from Operating Activities	

c) Prepare the Statement of Cash Flows for Garibaldi Ltd for the year ended 31st December 20X9.

	£000
Net Cash From Operating Activities	
Investing Activities	
Purchases of PPE	
Proceeds on Disposal of PPE	
Dividends Received	
Investment	
Net Cash Used in Investing Activities	
Financing Activities	
Increase in share capital	
Increase in loan	
Dividends paid	
Net Cash From Financing Activities	
Net increase / (decrease) in cash and cash equivalents	
Cash and cash equivalents at beginning of year	
Cash and cash equivalents at end of year	

Task 3 (8 marks)

a) The objective of Financial Statements, according to the IASB Conceptual Framework, is "to provide information about the reporting entity that is useful to existing and potential investors, lenders and other creditors in making decisions about providing resources to the entity".

Identify the two primary users of published financial statements, and, for each, explain the ways in which they will use them.

b) Explain the importance of the fundamental ethical concepts of Integrity and Professional Competence and Due Care when preparing financial statements.

Task 4 (12 marks)

Jammy Ltd is preparing its accounts for the year ended 31st December 20X2. The following matters have been brought to your attention.

a) During the year Jammy Ltd leased a machine for eight months. During the lease period, Jammy Ltd were responsible for maintaining the machine and for any repairs which became necessary. At the end of the eight months the machine was returned to the hire company, although Jammy Ltd could have extended the lease period had they wished.

Explain (with reasons) whether this should be treated as a finance lease or a short-term lease, and how it should be shown in the financial statements of Jammy Ltd.

b) On 16th January 20X3, Jammy Ltd was found guilty of breaches of employment law in a court case which had taken eight months to reach this conclusion. As a result, the company was fined £45,000.

Making reference to the relevant International Accounting Standard, explain how this should be accounted for in the financial statements for the year ended 31st December 20X2.

c) The directors of Jammy Ltd are considering spending £2,180,000 in the coming year on research and development expenditure. £1,190,000 of this will be on building a new sound measurement laboratory, and the remaining £990,000 on salaries and other costs. The company hope to develop a new product which will allow hearing aids to be made even smaller than they already are. The research is still at an early stage, and the directors estimate it could be several years before there is a saleable product. If technology advances quicker than the company's research, the whole project could be shelved, as competitors could bring a similar product to the market in a shorter timescale.

Explain, with reference to the relevant International Accounting Standard, how the forthcoming expenditure should be accounted for.

d) The directors of Jammy Ltd have identified a machine which originally cost £355,000 and which has been depreciated by £200,000 as at 31st December 20X2. Due to improvements in technology, the machine is now considered obsolete for the purposes for which it was originally acquired. The directors have identified that if they keep the machine, the discounted future cash flows which could be earned from it would amount to £150,000. There is no ready market for the machine in the UK, but it could be sold overseas for £190,000; however, Jammy Ltd would need to spend £42,000 to enable this sale to take place and to ship the machine overseas.

With reference to the relevant International Accounting Standard, identify whether the value of the machine has been impaired, and if so, how any impairment loss should be accounted for in the financial statements of Jammy Ltd.

e) Jammy Ltd has a 90% subsidiary company, Dodger Ltd. During the year Jammy Ltd sold goods to Dodger Ltd which had originally cost £23,000 for £38,000. At 31st December 20% of these goods remained unsold by Dodger Ltd.

Demonstrate how this transaction would be accounted for in the consolidated financial statements at 31st December 20X9.

Task 5 (30 marks)

The Managing Director of Rich Ltd has asked you to prepare the consolidated Statement of Financial Position for the group. Rich Ltd has one subsidiary undertaking, Tea Ltd. The Statements of Financial Position of the two companies as at 31 March 20X4 are set out below.

Balance sheets as at 31 March 20X4	Rich Ltd	Tea Ltd
	£000	**£000**
Non-current assets		
Property, plant and equipment	45,210	27,480
Investment in Tea Ltd	23,000	
	68,210	27,480
Current assets		
Inventories	21,450	4,222
Trade and other receivables	9,874	6,486
Cash and cash equivalents	1,458	127
	32,782	10,835
Total assets	**100,992**	**38,315**
Equity		
Share capital	38,000	12,000
Share premium	11,000	6,000
Retained earnings	22,526	11,740
Total equity	71,526	29,740
Non-current liabilities		
Long-term loans	14,000	4,000
Current liabilities		
Trade and other payables	11,234	4,445
Tax liabilities	4,232	130
	15,466	4,575
Total liabilities	29,466	8,575
Total Equity and Liabilities	**100,992**	**38,315**

Further information:

- The share capital of Tea Ltd consists of ordinary shares of £1 each. Ownership of these shares carries voting rights in Tea Ltd. There have been no changes to the balances of share capital and share premium during the year. No dividends were paid or proposed by Tea Ltd during the year.

- Rich Ltd acquired 7,200,000 shares in Tea Ltd on 1 April 20X3.
- On 1 April 20X3, the balance of retained earnings of Tea Ltd was £9,640,000.
- The fair value of the non-current assets of Tea Ltd at 1 April 20X3 was £29,800,000. The book value of the non-current assets at 1 April 20X3 was £25,800,000. The revaluation has not been recorded in the books of Tea Ltd (ignore any effect on the depreciation for the year).
- Included in Trade and other receivables for Rich Ltd and in Trade and other payables for Tea Ltd is an inter-company transaction for £3,000,000 that took place in early March 20X4.
- The directors of Rich plc have concluded that goodwill has been impaired by 25% during the year.

Complete the following workings boxes to calculate the correct figures for Goodwill, Retained Earnings and Non-Controlling Interest.

Goodwill	
	£000
Consideration	
Non-controlling Interest at acquisition	
Less: Net assets acquired	
Initial Goodwill	
Less: Impairment Adjustment	
Adjusted Goodwill	

Retained Earnings	
	£000
Rich Ltd	
Tea Ltd attributable to Rich Ltd	
Less: Impairment Adjustment	

Non-Controlling Interest (NCI)	
	£000
Share Capital attributable to NCI	
Share Premium attributable to NCI	
Retained Earnings attributable to NCI	
Revaluation Reserve attributable to NCI	
Non-Controlling Interest	

Draft the Consolidated Statement of Financial Position for Rich Ltd as at 31st March 20X4.

ASSETS	£000
Non-Current Assets	
Goodwill	
Property, Plant and Equipment	
Current Assets	
Inventories	
Trade Receivables	
Cash and Cash Equivalents	
Total Assets	
EQUITY AND LIABILITIES	
Equity	
Share Capital	
Share Premium	
Retained Earnings	
Non-Controlling Interest	
Total Equity	
Non-Current Liabilities	
Bank Loans	
Current Liabilities	
Trade Payables	
Taxation	
Total Liabilities	
Total Equity and Liabilities	

Task 6 (8 marks)

You have been given the financial statements of Bronco Ltd for the year ended 31 December 20X1. You are now required to prepare financial ratios to assist your manager in his analysis of the company.

Bronco Ltd's statement of profit or loss and statement of financial position are set out below.

Statement of Profit or Loss For the year ended 31 October 20X1	
	£0
Revenue	108,320
Cost of Sales	-58,520
GROSS PROFIT	**49,800**
Distribution Costs	-23,680
Administrative Expenses	-9,886
PROFIT FROM OPERATIONS	**16,234**
Finance Costs	-1,155
PROFIT BEFORE TAX	**15,079**
Tax	-3,560
PROFIT FOR YEAR FROM CONTINUING OPERATIONS	**11,519**

Statement of Financial Position	
ASSETS	**£0**
Non-Current Assets	
Property, Plant and Equipment	60,000
Current Assets	
Inventories	15,268
Trade and Other Receivables	11,752
Cash and Cash Equivalents	73
TOTAL ASSETS	**87,093**
EQUITY AND LIABILITIES	
Equity	
Share Capital	12,000
Share Premium	7,800
Retained Earnings	55,446
Total Equity	**75,246**
Non-current Liabilities	
Bank loans	2,600
Current Liabilities	
Trade and Other Payables	5,687
Tax Payable	3,560
Total Liabilities	**11,847**
TOTAL EQUITY AND LIABILITIES	**87,093**

Calculate the following ratios to ONE decimal place:

Gross profit percentage		%
Operating profit		%
ROCE		%
Asset turnover (net assets)		times

Task 7 (22 marks)

Jeremiah Bootfeather looking to invest in Cheesan Ltd. He wishes to assess the level of profitability and the level of risk of maintaining his investment in the company. He has asked you to assist him by analysing the financial statements of the company for the last two years. He has provided you with the following ratios.

	20X9	20X8
Gross profit percentage	27.50%	24.00%
Operating profit percentage	8.50%	12.00%
ROCE	8.6%	12.8%
Interest cover ratio	2.0 times	4.3 times

Prepare an email to your Jeremiah containing:

a) Whether the ratio is better or worse compared to the industry average and what it tells you about the performance of the company.

b) Based solely on the ratios given, what advice would you give to the investor (with reasons) as to whether the investor should buy the shares and invest in the company or not.

To:	Jeremiah Bootfeather
From:	AAT student
Subject:	Investment in Cheesan Ltd.

This page is left intentionally blank.

Chapter 1: Background to Financial Accounting - Answers

Task 1.1

a) What does IFRS stand for?

	✓
International Financial Reporting Standards	✓
International Financial Relationship Statistics	
Integrated Financial Reporting Standards	

b) Identify the objective of the IASB from the following options.

	✓
To develop and revise accounting standards in the UK	
To develop a single set of global accounting standards	✓
To develop and publish local accounting standards in every country	

c) What does GAAP stand for?

	✓
Globally Accepted Accounting Practice	
Generally Accepted Accounting Practice	✓
Global Accredited Accounting Practices	

d) Identify who issues the international financial reporting standards from the following options.

	✓
The Government	
The International Accounting Standards Board	✓
The IFRS Foundation	

Task 1.2

Identify if the following statement is true or false.

	✓
True	✓
False	

Task 1.3

Identify from the following the two underlying assumptions recognised by the conceptual framework?

	✓
Relevance	
Going concern	✓
Faithful representation	
Accruals basis	✓

Task 1.4

a) What are the two fundamental qualitative characteristics of useful information?

	✓
Timeliness	
Understandability	
Relevance	✓
Verifiability	
Faithful Representation	✓
Comparability	

b) What are the four enhancing qualitative characteristics?

	✓
Timeliness	✓
Understandability	✓
Relevance	
Verifiability	✓
Faithful Representation	
Comparability	✓

Task 1.5

a) Explain the meaning of the term 'relevance' based on the IFRS Conceptual Framework.

Information is relevant if it:

- *Is capable of making a difference in the decision-making process.*

And either

- *Has predictive value – it allows the user to make predictions about future events, or*
- *Has confirmatory value – it allows the user to confirm past evaluations.*

b) Explain the meaning of the term 'verifiability' based on the IFRS Conceptual Framework.

Verifiability means that the information (and the original sources of it) can be checked and verified – this provides greater assurance to the user that it is both credible and reliable.

Task 1.6

Match the following descriptions to the correct accounting concepts.

Choose from: The business entity concept, Consistency, Materiality, Prudence.

Description	Concept
No information or items should be omitted or misstated that could reasonably impact or influence the decisions of the primary users of the financial statements.	**Materiality**
The financial statements are prepared purely from the perspective of the business – they do not include any valuations of personal assets or liabilities of the owners.	**The business entity concept**
Adopting a cautious approach when preparing financial statements. Gains or profits should only be recognised in the accounts when they have actually been made, whilst losses should be recorded as soon as it becomes probable they will arise.	**Prudence**
Financial statements should be prepared using the same accounting techniques and valuation bases as previous statements – this is to help make the statements more comparable over time.	**Consistency**

Task 1.7

a) Which key piece of legislation requires limited companies to file annual financial statements?

	✓
The Partnership Act 1890	
The Companies Act 2006	✓
The Corporate Law Rules 2021	

b) Identify from the following the criteria that must be met for a limited company to be exempt from being audited.

	✓
An annual turnover of no more than £10.2 million	✓
An annual turnover of no more than £8 million	
Assets worth no more than £5.1 million	✓
50 or fewer employees on average	✓
Assets worth no more than £7 million	

c) Identify which of the following must be presented by limited companies.

	✓
A Statement of Profit or Loss and Other Comprehensive Income	✓
A Statement of Changes in Equity	✓
A Statement of Financial Position	✓
A Statement of Cash Flows	✓
A Directors' Report	✓
Appropriation Account	
Group (Consolidated) Accounts where a company has subsidiaries	✓
Capital Accounts	

Task 1.8

State what information each of the following financial statements provides for users.

Statement of Profit or Loss and Other Comprehensive Income
Shows the performance over the last period and other gains and losses.

Statement of Financial Position
Shows the assets and liabilities along with the financial health and strength of the business.

Statement of Cash Flows
Shows the financial adaptability and the cash flows in and out of the business.

Statement of Changes in Equity
Provides an explanation of the changes in the equity section of the statement of financial position since the start of the accounting period.

Task 1.9

a) What are the elements of the Statement of Financial Position?

	✓
Assets	✓
Expenses	
Sales	
Equity	✓
Liabilities	✓
Purchases	

b) What is the accounting equation that the Statement of Financial position is based on?

Assets	=	**Equity**	+	**Liabilities**

Task 1.10

The conceptual framework defines the five elements of the financial statements.

Write the definitions of each element in the spaces below.

Definition of an Asset
An asset is "a present economic resource controlled by the entity as a result of past events. An economic resource is a right that has the potential to produce economic benefits".

Definition of a Liability
A liability is "a present obligation of the entity to transfer an economic resource as a result of past events".

Definition of Equity
Equity is "the owners' residual interest in the assets of the entity, after deducting all its liabilities".

Definition of Income
Income is "Increases in assets or decreases in liabilities that result in increase in equity, other than those relating to contributions from holders of equity claims.

Definition of Expense
Expenses are "Decreases in assets or increases in liabilities that result in decreases in equity, other than those relating to distributions to holders of equity claims.

Chapter 2: Financial Statements of Limited Companies - Answers

Task 2.1

Identify which of the following businesses are unincorporated or incorporated.

	Unincorporated / Incorporated
Sole trader	**Unincorporated**
Private limited company	**Incorporated**
Limited liability partnership	**Incorporated**
Public limited company	**Incorporated**
Partnership	**Unincorporated**

Task 2.2

Identify which of the following statements are true.

	✓
Sole traders have limited liability and their personal assets are not assets at risk.	
Shareholders have limited liability and are only liable to lose the amount they originally invested if the business fails.	✓
Sole traders and partners take dividends from the profits of the business.	
Shareholders appoint directors for the day to day running of the business.	✓
Limited companies pay Corporation Tax on their profits and must file a copy of their financial statements to Companies House each year.	✓
Directors cannot also be shareholders of a company.	
Public limited companies can offer shares to the general public to raise capital.	✓

Task 2.3

Identify which of the following relate to limited companies only.

	✓
Owners are not involved in the day-to-day management of the business.	✓
Filing annual financial statements at companies house every year is not required.	
Annual financial statements must be prepared in line with the accounting standards.	✓
The owners' *equity* is made up of the amounts they have originally invested, retained earnings and other gains and losses.	✓
Limited companies pay corporation tax on their profits.	✓
The owners of the business will take money out of the business through drawings.	

Task 2.4

Match each of the following stakeholders to whether they are internal or external.

Stakeholder	Internal ✓	External ✓
Investors		✓
Managers	✓	
Lenders		✓
Shareholders	✓	
Staff	✓	
The Government		✓
Local communities		✓
Customers / Suppliers		✓

Task 2.5

Describe three main differences between the financial statements of sole traders and limited companies?

There are three main differences:

Capital and retained earnings: capital invested by shareholders is classified as share capital (nominal value) and share premium. Retained earnings are retained profits, bought forward from the previous year, plus the net profit for the year, minus any dividends paid. The amounts relating to retained earnings are stated in the statement of changes in equity.

Dividends: these are the same as drawings for sole traders. These are only recognised when they are paid for cash purposes.

Tax: Tax does not appear in the SPL of the sole traders, however it does with limited companies. Corporation tax will be charged to the SPL as an expense for limited companies.

Other possible differences:

Notes: Limited companies have a set of notes as part of their financial statements. These are normally set out as required by the accounting standards. Any workings are not published with the accounts and are kept confidential.

Non-current assets: PPE appears as only the carrying amount in the SFP for limiting companies. These are analysed in the notes of the accounts.

Expenses in the SPL of limited companies are grouped together into distribution costs and administrative expenses. The SPL of sole traders lists the expenses.

Task 2.6

A company has calculated the value of its closing inventories at the year end at £450,000. It has subsequently realised that goods included in this figure which had been valued at £40,000 were in fact only able to sold for £10,000 due to damage.

What is the revised value of the inventory for inclusion in the Statement of Financial Position at the year end?

£420,000

Task 2.7

Identify which of the following items would be shown in the Statement of Profit or Loss and Other comprehensive Income or the Statement of Financial Position.

	In SPLOCI	In SFP
Ordinary Share Capital		✓
Share Premium Reserve		✓
Revaluation Reserve		✓
Administrative Expenses	✓	
Trade and Other Payables		✓
Retained earnings		✓
Distribution Costs	✓	
Land and buildings – at cost		✓
Plant and equipment – at cost		✓
Land and buildings – accumulated depreciation		✓
Plant and equipment – accumulated depreciation		✓
Trade and Other Receivables		✓
Accruals		✓
Prepayments		✓
Bank Loan		✓
Interest Paid	✓	
Sales	✓	
Purchases	✓	
Inventories at start of the year	✓	
Sales Returns	✓	
Purchase Returns	✓	
Provision for Doubtful Debts		✓
Final Dividend		✓
Cash & Cash Equivalents		✓
Inventories at the end of the year	✓	✓
Tax charge for the year	✓	
Interim Dividend		✓

Task 2.8

Fusion-Tech Ltd

a) Draft the statement of profit or loss and other comprehensive income for Fusion-Tech Ltd for the year ended 30 November 20X3.

b) Draft the statement of financial position for Fusion-Tech Ltd as at 30 November 20X3. Use the workings boxes to help you.

Fusion-Tech Ltd Statement of Profit or Loss and Other Comprehensive Income for the year ended 30 November 20X3	
	£000
Revenue	29,873
Cost of Sales	-14,635
Gross profit	15,238
Distribution Costs	-3,987
Administrative Expenses	-2,669
Operating profit	8,582
Finance Costs	-492
Profit before tax	8,090
Tax	-934
Profit for the period from continuing operations	7,156
Other Comprehensive Income	-
Total comprehensive income for the year	7,156

Workings boxes:

Cost of Sales	£000
Opening Inventories	4,245
Purchases	15,664
Closing Inventories	-5,274
Total	14,635

Administrative Expenses	£000
Administrative expenses	2,687
Prepayment *(27 / 12 x 8)*	-18
Total	2,669

Note: Interest on the loan for year = £8,200,000 x 6% = £492,000.
Only £246,000 of this has been accounted for so we need to set up an accrual for £246,000.

Fusion-Tech Ltd Statement of Financial Position as at 30 November 20X3	
	£000
ASSETS	
Non-Current Assets	
Property, Plant and Equipment	18,591
Current Assets	
Inventories	5,274
Trade and Other Receivables	5,928
Cash and Cash Equivalents	1,166
TOTAL ASSETS	30,959
EQUITY AND LIABILITIES	
Equity	
Share Capital	6,000
Retained Earnings	12,820
Total Equity	18,802
Non-current Liabilities	
Bank loans	8,200
Current Liabilities	
Trade and Other Payables	3,005
Tax Payable	934
Total Liabilities	12,139
TOTAL EQUITY AND LIABILITIES	30,959

Workings boxes:

Trade and Other Receivables	£000
Trade and other receivables	3,660
Prepayment	18
Credit sales	2,250
Total	5,928

Retained Earnings	£000
Retained earnings	6,784
Profit for the year	7,156
Dividends paid	-1,120
Total	12,820

Trade and Other Payables	£000
Trade and other payables	2,526
Accruals	233
Interest accrual	246
Total	3,005

Task 2.9

Eco-Verse Ltd

a) Draft the statement of profit or loss and other comprehensive income for Eco-Verse Ltd for the year ended year ended 31 October 20X2.

b) Draft the statement of financial position for Eco-Verse Ltd year ended 31 October 20X2.

Use the workings boxes to help you.

Eco-Verse Ltd **Statement of Profit or Loss and Other Comprehensive Income for the year ended 31 October 20X2**	
	£000
Revenue	38,201
Cost of Sales	-20,235
Gross profit	17,966
Distribution Costs	-3,289
Administrative Expenses	-3,391
Operating profit	11,286
Finance Costs	-720
Profit before tax	10,566
Tax	-1,520
Profit for the period from continuing operations	9,046
Other Comprehensive Income	-
Total comprehensive income for the year	9,046

Workings boxes:

Cost of Sales	£000
Opening Inventories	4,586
Purchases	18,250
Closing Inventories	-3,939
Depreciation	1,338
Total	20,235

Distribution Costs	£000
Distribution Costs	2,834
Depreciation	446
Accruals	9
Total	3,289

Administrative Expenses	£000
Administrative expenses	2,945
Depreciation	446
Total	3,391

Depreciation workings:

Land and Buildings: 25,200 – 8,200 land = 17,000 x 2% ***= 340***

Plant & Equipment: 13,250 – 3,800 accumulated dep = 9,450 x 20% = ***1,890***

Total Depreciation for the year: 340 + 1,890 = ***2,230***

60% to COS: 2,230 x 60% = ***1,338***

20% to Distribution Costs: 2,230 x 20% = ***446***

20% to Administrative Expenses: 2,230 x 20% = ***446***

Eco-Verse Ltd Statement of Financial Position as at 31 October 20X2	
	£000
ASSETS	
Non-Current Assets	
Property, Plant and Equipment	28,420
Current Assets	
Inventories	3,939
Trade and Other Receivables	3,098
Cash and Cash Equivalents	5,280
TOTAL ASSETS	**40,737**
EQUITY AND LIABILITIES	
Equity	
Share Capital	15,000
Retained Earnings	11,672
Total Equity	**26,672**
Non-current Liabilities	
Bank loans	9,000
Current Liabilities	
Trade and Other Payables	3,545
Tax Payable	1,520
Total Liabilities	**14,065**
TOTAL EQUITY AND LIABILITIES	**40,737**

Workings boxes:

PPE	£000
Land and buildings at cost	25,200
Accumulated depreciation – land and buildings *(4,000 + 340)*	-4,340
Plant and equipment at cost	13,250
Accumulated depreciation of plant and equipment *(3,800 + 1,890)*	-5,690
Total	**28,420**

Retained Earnings	£000
Retained earnings	3,926
Profit for the year	9,046
Dividends paid	-1,300
Total	11,672

Trade and Other Payables	£000
Trade and other payables	2,894
Accruals (from TB)	282
Distribution accrual	9
Interest accrual	360
Total	3,545

Task 2.10

Dickinson Distribution Ltd

a) Draft the statement of profit or loss and other comprehensive income for Dickinson Distribution Ltd for the year ended year ended 31 December 20X4.

b) Draft the statement of financial position for Dickinson Distribution Ltd year ended 31 December 20X4.

Use the workings boxes to help you.

Dickinson Distribution Ltd Statement of Profit or Loss and Other Comprehensive Income for the year ended 31 December 20X4	
	£000
Revenue	12,734
Cost of Sales	-6,665
Gross profit	6,069
Distribution Costs	-1,311
Administrative Expenses	-1,210
Operating profit	3,548
Finance Costs	-240
Profit before tax	3,308
Tax	-308
Profit for the period from continuing operations	3,000
Other Comprehensive Income	-
Total comprehensive income for the year	3,000

Workings boxes:

Cost of Sales	£000
Opening Inventories	1,529
Purchases	6,083
Closing Inventories	-1,313
Depreciation	366
Total	6,665

Administrative Expenses	£000
Administrative expenses	982
Depreciation	183
Irrecoverable debts	45
Total	1,210

Distribution Costs	£000
Distribution Costs	945
Depreciation	366
Total	1,311

Depreciation workings:

Land and Buildings: *8,400 – 2,700 land = 5,700 x 5%* **= 285**

Plant & Equipment: *4,417 – 1,267 accumulated dep= 3,150 x 20%* = **630**

Total Depreciation for the year: *285 + 630* = **915**

40% to COS: *915 x 40%* = **366**

40% to Distribution Costs: *915 x 40%* = **366**

20% to Administrative Expenses: *915 x 20%* = **183**

Dickinson Distribution Ltd Statement of Financial Position as at 31 October 20X2	
	£000
ASSETS	
Non-Current Assets	
Property, Plant and Equipment	9,302
Current Assets	
Inventories	1313
Trade and Other Receivables	988
Cash and Cash Equivalents	1,760
TOTAL ASSETS	13,363
EQUITY AND LIABILITIES	
Equity	
Share Capital	5,000
Retained Earnings	3,876
Total Equity	8,876
Non-current Liabilities	
Bank loans	3,000
Current Liabilities	
Trade and Other Payables	1,179
Tax Payable	308
Total Liabilities	4,487
TOTAL EQUITY AND LIABILITIES	13,363

Workings boxes:

PPE	£000
Land and buildings at cost	8,400
Accumulated depreciation – land and buildings *(1,333 + 285)*	-1,618
Plant and equipment at cost	4,417
Accumulated depreciation of plant and equipment *(1,267 + 630)*	-1,897
Total	9,302

Trade and Other Receivables	£000
Trade and other receivables	1,033
Irrecoverable debt	-45
Total	988

Retained Earnings	£000
Retained earnings	1,309
Profit for the year	3,000
Dividends paid	-433
Total	3,876

Trade and Other Payables	£000
Trade and other payables	965
Accruals	94
Interest accrual	120
Total	1,179

Chapter 3: Equity - Answers

Task 3.1

a) Identify the correct items that are included in the 'Equity' section of the Statement of Financial Position for limited companies.

	✓
Share capital	✓
Capital account	
Revaluation reserve	✓
Retained earnings	✓
Share premium	✓
Assets	

b) Identify the two major classes of shares in limited companies from the following options.

	✓
Ordinary shares	✓
Selection shares	
Possession shares	
Preference shares	✓

Task 3.2

a) Explain what is meant by the term 'bonus shares'.

Bonus shares are an issue of new shares to existing shareholders at no cost – the shareholder simply receives a number of 'free' shares. A bonus issue does not therefore raise any additional funds for the company.

b) Explain what is meant by the term 'rights issue' in relation to shares.

A rights issue is an offer made to existing shareholders to buy more shares at a discounted rate. This is done to reward existing shareholders, and may also make it easier for the company to sell the required number of shares in order to raise the required funds.

The maximum number of shares each shareholder can buy is determined by the size of their current shareholding. For example, in a 2 for 1 offer, shareholders can purchase 2 new shares for every share that they already own.

Task 3.3

Marine Manufacturing Ltd issued 10,000 shares for £1.50 each. The nominal value of the shares is 50p.

a) Calculate the amount to be entered in the share capital account and the share premium account.

Share Capital:	£	**5,000**
Share Premium:	£	**10,000**

b) What would be the account treatment for this?

Account name	Dr or Cr	Amount
Cash received (bank)	**Dr**	**£15,000**
Share capital	**Cr**	**£5,000**
Share premium	**Cr**	**£10,000**

Task 3.4

a) Calculate the total number of issued shares after the bonus issue.

Original issue	=	**10,000 shares**
Bonus Issue	=	**2,500 shares** *(10,000 x 1/4)*
Total	=	**12,500 shares**

b) Show the double entry to record the bonus issue.

	Account	£
Dr	**Share Premium A/c**	**£2,500**
Cr	**Ordinary Share Capital**	**£2,500**

c) Complete the equity section of the Statement of Financial Position.

Equity (extract)	
Ordinary shares	**12,500**
Share premium	**4,500**
Retained earnings	**128,000**
Total equity	**145,000**

Task 3.5

Katerina Catering Ltd has property that has been revalued and it has increased in value. This must be recognised in the accounts of the business. Identify whether the following entries will be a debit or credit to record this increase.

	DR / CR
Property at cost	**DR**
Accumulated depreciation	**DR**
Revaluation reserve	**CR**

Task 3.6

A company made a share issue during the year of 160,000 ordinary £1 shares, raising £260,000. How is this shown in the Statement of Changes in Equity?

	✓
It should not be recorded in the Statement of Changes in Equity	
Include £260,000 in Share Capital	
Include £160,000 in Share Capital and £100,000 in Revaluation Reserve	
Include £160,000 in Share Capital and £100,000 in Share Premium Reserve	✓

Task 3.7

a) Complete the following sentence.

Any profits not paid out in the form of dividends are called **retained earnings**.

b) Calculate the retained earnings to be included in the Statement of Financial position for the year ended 31 December 20X4.

Retained Earnings	£000
Retained earnings at 1 Jan 20X4	1,234
Profit for the period	840
Dividends paid	650
Retained earnings at 31 December 20X4	**1,424**

Task 3.8

What would the double entry be to record this?

Account	Dr or Cr	Amount
Property at cost	Dr	£6,000,000
Accumulated Depreciation	Dr	£2,500,000
Revaluation reserve	Cr	£8,500,000

Task 3.9

Prepare the Statement of Changes in Equity for the year ended 31st December 20X4.

	Share Capital	Share Premium	Revaluation Reserve	Retained Earnings	Total Equity
	£000	£000	£000	£000	£000
Balance at start of year	300	70	0	285	655
Changes in Equity:					
Comprehensive Income			250	630	880
Dividends				-300	-300
Issue of Share Capital	60	40			100
Balance at end of year	360	110	250	615	1335

Task 3.10

Sharp Manufacturing Ltd

a) Draft the statement of profit or loss and other comprehensive income for Sharp Manufacturing Ltd for the year ended 31 December 20X4.

b) Draft the statement of financial position for Sharp Manufacturing Ltd as at 31 December 20X4.

Sharp Manufacturing Ltd **Statement of Profit or Loss and Other Comprehensive Income for the year ended 31 December 20X4**	
	£000
Revenue	9,594
Cost of Sales	-5,880
Gross profit	3,714
Distribution Costs	-883
Administrative Expenses	-1,572
Operating profit	1,259
Finance Costs	-70
Profit before tax	1,189
Tax	-231
Profit for the period from continuing operations	958
Other Comprehensive Income	-
Total comprehensive income for the year	958

Workings boxes:

Cost of Sales	£000
Opening Inventories	1,034
Purchases	5,771
Closing Inventories	-925
Total	5,880

Administrative Expenses	£000
Administrative expenses	1,601
Salary	-55
Irrecoverable debt	26
Total	1,572

Distribution Costs	£000
Distribution Costs	812
Accrual	16
Salary	55
Total	883

Sharp Manufacturing Ltd Statement of Financial Position as at 31 December 20X4	
	£000
ASSETS	
Non-Current Assets	
Property, Plant and Equipment	5,092
Current Assets	
Inventories	925
Trade and Other Receivables	809
Cash and Cash Equivalents	61
TOTAL ASSETS	6,887
EQUITY AND LIABILITIES	
Equity	
Share Capital	3,564
Retained Earnings	1,386
Total Equity	*4,950
Non-current Liabilities	
Bank loans	985
Current Liabilities	
Trade and Other Payables	721
Tax Payable	231
Total Liabilities	1,937
TOTAL EQUITY AND LIABILITIES	6,887

Workings boxes:

Trade and Other Receivables	£000
Trade and other receivables	746
Prepayment	89
Irrecoverable debt	-26
Total	809

Retained Earnings	£000
Retained earnings	703
Profit for the year	958
Dividends paid	275
Total	1,386

Trade and Other Payables	£000
Trade and other payables	705
Accruals	16
Total	721

c) Draft the Statement of Changes in Equity for Sharp Manufacturing Ltd as at 31 December 20X4.

	Share Capital	Revaluation Surplus	Retained Earnings	Total Equity
	£000	£000	£000	£000
Balance at start of year	3,564	0	703	4,267
Changes in Equity:				
Comprehensive Income			958	958
Dividends			-275	-275
Issue of Share Capital	0			0
Balance at end of year	3,564	0	1,386	*4,950

**Note: The total balance of total equity at the end of the year balances with the Total Equity section in the Statement of Financial Position.*

This page is left intentionally blank.

Chapter 4: Assets - Answers

Task 4.1

a) Identify which of the following are current or non-current assets.

Assets	Current / Non-current
Trade receivables	Current
Prepayments	Current
Land	Non-Current
Vehicles	Non-Current
Cash and cash equivalents	Current
Inventories	Current
Plant and machinery	Non-Current
Office equipment	Non-Current

b) Identify which of the following are characteristics of a non-current asset.

	✓
Must be tangible	
Can be tangible and intangible	✓
Is expected to be used over more than one period of 12 months	✓
Is expected to be used within one period of 12 months	

c) Identify which International Accounting Standard deals with the tangible assets of Plant, Property and Equipment.

	✓
IAS 2	
IAS 16	✓
IAS 36	
IAS 37	

Task 4.2

a) Identify which of the following IAS 16 considers when dealing with non-current assets.

	✓
Impairment of assets	
When to recognise an asset	✓
How to record the carrying value of an asset	✓
How to record leased assets	
When and how to depreciate non-current assets	✓
Intangible assets	

b) Which two criteria must be met when identifying whether an asset should be recognised in the financial statements?

1. It is probable that future economic benefits will flow to the entity.
2. The cost of the asset must be reliably measured.

c) Companies are permitted to value their assets on two bases. Identify which model the following descriptions relate to.

	Model
Where non-current assets are revalued periodically, and revalued at their 'fair value' less any subsequent accumulated depreciation.	**Revaluation**
Where non-current assets are valued at their historic cost, less accumulated depreciation.	**Cost**

d) Identify which of the following statements is **false**.

	✓
If an entity chooses to adopt the revaluation model, then all assets in the same class must be valued using this basis.	
If an entity chooses to adopt the revaluation model, then only that particular asset must be valued using this basis.	✓
Under the revaluation model, assets of that class must be revalued regularly to ensure the carrying amount of the asset does not materially differ from its fair value stated in the financial statements.	
If an entity chooses to adopt the revaluation model for a class of asset, then other classes of assets can continue to use the cost model.	

Task 4.3

a) Where an asset is revalued upwards, what are the accounting entries to record this?

DR **Asset**
CR **Revaluation Reserve**

b) Where would this appear in the financial statements?

	✓
Increase Non-Current Assets (SFP)	✓
Other Comprehensive Income (SPL)	✓
Revenue as additional income (SPL)	
Equity section (SFP)	✓
Non-Current Liabilities (SFP)	

c) Which of the following costs could be included in the cost of a new industrial drilling machine?

a) Costs of site preparation. ✓

b) Costs of testing the asset before being brought into use. ✓

c) Cost of professional fees (e.g. architect or surveyor). ✓

d) Cost of ongoing maintenance contract for the machine

e) Cost of initial delivery of the machine. ✓

f) Cost of replacement drill pieces for the machine

d) Calculate the depreciation expense recognised in the Statement of Profit of Loss and the carrying amount of the asset to be recorded in the Statement of Financial Position as at 31st December 20X3 using:

i) Straight line method.

	Depreciation for the year (SPL)	Carrying Amount (SFP)
31/12/20X1	*(£200,000 - £10,000) / 5* = **£38,000**	*£200,000 - £38,000* = **£162,000**
31/12/20X2	*(£200,000 - £10,000) / 5* = **£38,000**	*£162,000 - £38,000* = **£124,000**
31/12/20X3	*(£200,000 - £10,000) / 5* = **£38,000**	*£124,000 - £38,000* = **£86,000**

ii) Diminishing / reducing balance method at 20% per annum.

	Depreciation for the year (SPL)	Carrying Amount (SFP
31/12/20X1	*£200,000 x 20%=* **£40,000**	*£200,000 - £40,000* = **£160,000**
31/12/20X2	£160,000 x 20% = **£32,000**	*£160,000 - £32,000* = **£128,000**
31/12/20X3	£128,000 x 20% = **£25,600**	*£128,000 - £25,600* = **£102,400**

Task 4.4

a) Complete the following sentences.

Choose from: controls, lease, Lessee, Lessor, right of use, own.

A business does not necessarily have to ***own*** an item for it to be considered an asset; it may be enough that it simply ***controls*** the item.

A lease contract is an agreement between the ***Lessor*** (who owns the asset) and the ***Lessee*** (who leases the asset).

The lessee has the ***right of use*** of the asset in exchange for payment made to the lessor.

b) Is the following statement true or false?

A contract is, or contains, a lease if it conveys the right to control the use of an identified asset for the period of time in exchange for consideration.

	✓
True	✓
False	

c) Complete the following sentences.

Choose from: past, present, current, increase, decrease, completely, partially.

A lease liability will be recognised at the ***present*** value of the minimum lease payments. This liability will then ***decrease*** over the lease period until it has been ***completely*** repaid by the end of the agreement.

Task 4.5

Axel Ltd is a parts manufacturer. In Axel Ltd's latest financial year, it entered a number of lease agreements for assets as below. For each, you should identify whether it should be treated as a **short term lease, low value asset lease** or a **lease**.

Leases	Type
Leased a packing machine on a 10 month lease. The value of the machine is £7,000.	**Short term lease**
Leased a van for making small deliveries on a three year lease. The list price of the van at the time of the lease is £16,000. The lease payments are agreed at £460 per month for the duration of the lease.	**Lease**
Leased a machine on a four year contract. At the end of the four-year period Axel Ltd will own the asset.	**Lease**
Leased a photocopier / printer. The term of the lease is 2 years and the value of the printer is £1,500.	**Low value asset lease**

Task 4.6

What entries will be entered into the Statement of Profit or Loss at the end of the year. Round your answers to the nearest whole pound.

Entry	£	Workings
Depreciation charges	**3,723**	**37,230 / 10 years**
Finance costs	**1,362**	**(37,230 – 10,000) x 5%**

Depreciated over the useful life as ownership passes to the lessee at end of lease term

Identify the entries to be entered into the Statement of Financial Position at the end of the year?

Entry	£	Workings
PPE	**33,507**	**37,230 – 3,723***
Lease Liability	**28,592**	**37,230 - 10,000 + 1,362**

How will the lease liability be split between the non-current liabilities and the current liabilities in the Statement of Financial Position?

	£
Non-current Liability	**18,592**
Current Liability	**10,000**

Task 4.7

a) Identify the relevant accounting standard and an explanation on how they will need to be treated these in the financial statements.

IFRS 16 relates to the treatment of leases. It requires all leased items to be initially recognised as assets in the financial statements of the user.

Leased assets are recognised at their fair value and depreciated over the length of the lease.

The lease liability is recognised at the present value of the minimum lease payments. This liability will then decrease over the lease period until it has been completely repaid by the end of the agreement.

Therefore, the vans would be treated as normal leased items and will therefore be recognised as assets by along with a corresponding liability.

The photocopier will be classed as a short life asset.

It is classified as a short life asset because the item is leased for a year or less. These are not recognised by the user as an asset or a liability. The lease payments are instead recognised as expenses in the Statement of Profit or Loss.

b) Explain how the lease should be recognised in the financial statements of Vanguard Ltd for the year ended 31 March 20X7. Show your calculations to illustrate your answer.

On the 1 April 20X6 the machinery should initially be recognised at the present value of the lease payments, as an asset and a lease liability of £29,384.

The asset should then be depreciated over 4 years. The depreciation charge for the year would be £7,346. (£29,384 / 4)

The carrying amount of the asset will be recognised in the Statement of Financial Position on the 31 March 20X7 as £22,038. (£29,384 - £7,346)

The interest expense will be recognised in the Statement of Profit or Loss as £1,763 (£29,384 x 6%).

The lease liability will be recognised in the Statement of Financial Position as £23,147 (£29,384 + £1,763 - £8,000).

Task 4.8

a) Identify which International Accounting Standard deals with the impairment of assets.

	✓
IAS 2	
IAS 16	
IAS 36	✓
IAS 37	

b) Details of the value of the machine are as follows:

What amount should be recognised for the machine in the Statement of Financial Position?

£43,200

*IAS 36 states that if an asset is impaired, it is to be included in the Statement of Financial of Position at its **recoverable amount** (the higher of fair value less costs to sell and the value in use).*

What is the amount of impairment loss that will be recognised in the Statement of Profit or Loss?

£10,800

The impairment amount will be included in the Statement of Profit or Loss. The value in use is £43,200. The value in use is higher so this is the recoverable amount. The impairment is £54,000 – £43,200 = £10,800.

c) Which of the assets have become impaired?

i) 1
ii) 2
iii) 1 and 2
iv) 1 and 3
v) 2 and 3 ✓

The carrying amounts of these assets are higher than their recoverable amount.

What is the impairment amount to be included in the Statement of Profit or Loss?

£13,500

The carry amount will need to be reduced to its recoverable value.

(37,500 – 34,000 = 3,500) + (75,000 – 65,000 = 10,000)

Task 4.9

a) Identify which of the following best describes an intangible asset under IAS 38.

	✓
An identifiable, non-monetary asset without physical form.	✓
An identifiable, monetary asset with physical form.	

b) Complete the following sentences.

Choose from: depreciation, discretion, accumulation, definite, indefinite.

Amortisation is the same as ***depreciation***, however amortisation only applies to intangible assets.

Intangible assets with a ***definite*** useful life are subject to amortisation. Intangible assets with an ***indefinite*** useful life are not subject to amortisation but instead are reviewed annually for impairment.

c) Identify which of the following are examples of intangible assets.

	✓
Goodwill	✓
Inventory	
Development costs	✓
Trade marks, licences, patents	✓
Computer equipment	
Vehicles	

d) Identify which of the following statements are true.

	✓
Internally generated brands cannot be recognised as an intangible asset because they cannot be measured reliably.	✓
Intangible assets which meet the recognition criteria should never be shown in the Statement of Financial Position.	
Intangible assets which meet the recognition criteria should be shown in the Statement of Financial Position at their original cost.	✓
Indefinite life intangible assets are not amortised, instead they are reviewed for impairment and if a finite life can be established.	✓
Intangible assets with an indefinite life must be amortised over that life on a systematic basis.	

Write a short email to Danica and outline what the criteria is for development expenditure to be capitalised in accordance with IAS 38 Intangible Assets.

Good afternoon Danica,

We would write off research and development expenditure to the Statement of Profit or Loss. However, if the development expenditure meets ALL of the following the criteria, then it may be capitalised in the financial statements.

The criteria requirements for development expenditure to be capitalised are as follows:

a) Probable future revenues/economic benefits will be generated from it.
b) Intention to complete it.
c) Resources are available to complete it.
d) Ability to use or sell it.
e) Technically feasible to complete it.
f) Expenditure that can be identified separately or can be reliably measured.

Task 4.10

a) Identify from the following what inventories must be valued at, under IAS 2.

	✓
The higher of cost and net realisable value.	
The lower of cost and net realisable value.	✓
The higher of the indirect cost and incurred cost.	
The lower of present value and original cost.	

b) Identify from the following which costs should be included in the cost of inventories?

	✓
Selling costs	
Transportation costs to the warehouse	✓
Import costs	✓
Storage and distribution costs	

c) Calculate the value of the inventory be stated as in the financial statements according to IAS 2 Inventories.

£77,200

IAS 2 only permits the use of FIFO and AVCO as methods of valuing inventory. IAS 2 also states inventory should only be measured at the lower of cost and net realisable value.

d) In accordance with IAS 2 Inventories, what is the value of the closing inventories to be recognised in the financial statements?

£117,120

Inventories are valued at the lower of cost and NRV. NRV = Selling price – selling costs (26,160 + 51,840 + 39,120).

Chapter 5: Other Accounting Standards - Answers

Task 5.1

a) Select the correct international accounting standard that deals with events after the reporting period.

	✓
IAS 2	
IAS 16	
IAS 10	✓
IAS 37	

Task 5.2

Complete the following sentences.

Choose from: adjust, IAS 10, IAS 38, events, impact, reporting, time.

There is a 'window' of time between when the ***reporting*** period has ended and when the financial statements have been finalised and authorised.

During this time ***events*** could occur that could have an ***impact*** on the information contained within those financial statements.

IAS 10 provides guidance on when an entity should ***adjust*** its financial statements for events after the reporting period.

Task 5.3

Identify which of the following best describes a material adjusting event and a material non-adjusting event.

Description	Adjusting / Non-adjusting
Is accounted for by altering the amounts shown in the financial statements to reflect the event.	**Adjusting**
Is not included by amending the financial statements. Instead, it is included as a note to the accounts giving, where possible, an indication of the likely financial effect of the event.	**Non adjusting**

Task 5.4

Ramana Ltd is preparing its financial statements to 31st December 20X4. The following events occurred in January 20X5, before the financial statements had been authorised.

Identify from the following which are adjusting events and non-adjusting events.

Events	Adjusting / Non-adjusting
Damage to non-current assets or loss of production due to fire or flood.	**Non adjusting**
Impairment of assets.	**Adjusting**
A reduction in value of inventories where net realisable value falls below cost.	**Adjusting**
Issue of new share capital.	**Non adjusting**
Discovery of fraud by an employee.	**Adjusting**
The major purchase of non-current assets.	**Non adjusting**
Conclusion of a court case which had been ongoing at the financial year end.	**Adjusting**
A new business combination – purchase of, or sale to, another entity.	**Non adjusting**
Insolvency of a major trade customer.	**Adjusting**
Taking out a new (or increasing an existing) loan.	**Non adjusting**

Task 5.5

a) Identify if there has been an over provision or an under provision for the year ended 31 March 20X4.

	✓
Over provision	✓
Under provision	

b) Calculate the tax charge that Centurion Ltd will show in the Statement of Profit or Loss and Other Comprehensive Income for the year ended 31st March 20X5.

£90,000

Over provision: £85,000 - £75,000 = £10,000
Tax charge: £100,000 - £10,000 = £90,000

c) Calculate the tax liability that will be shown in the Statement of Financial Position as at the 31 March 20X5.

£100,000

Task 5.6

Calculate the amount that should be included in the statement of profit or loss for the year ended 31 December 20X8.

£37,000

Task 5.7

Identify the relevant accounting standard that needs to be applied and how this should be recognised in the financial statements.

IFRS 15 - Revenue from Contracts with Customers.

Revenue should only be recognised when the performance obligation has been fulfilled, or at least partly fulfilled. As these items are still being made, the deposits cannot be recognised as sales. The deposits should be recognised as a current liability as deferred income (as if they owe the customers this money back).

Task 5.8

a) Identify the accounting treatment for contingent liabilities based on the likelihood of the event occurring. Choose from: Make provision, disclose in notes or ignore.

Event	Treatment
Almost certain	**Make provision**
Probable	**Make provision**
Possible	**Disclose in the notes**
Remote	**Ignore**

b) Identify the accounting treatment for contingent assets based on the likelihood of the event occurring. Choose from: Recognise, disclose in notes or ignore.

Event	Treatment
Almost certain	**Recognise**
Probable	**Disclose in the notes**
Possible	**Ignore**
Remote	**Ignore**

c) Identify if the following statements are true or false.

Event	True / False
A contingent asset is never shown in the financial statements if it is probable the event will occur, it will only be disclosed in the notes.	**True**
A contingent liability occurs when the event is possible but not probable.	**True**
A contingent liability occurs when the event is probable.	**False**
If a contingent asset is only possible or remote it should be ignored.	**True**
A contingent asset should be disclosed in the notes at all times.	**False**

Task 5.9

Explain whether the legal claim should be treated as a provision or a contingent liability and how it should be treated in the financial statements.

It should be treated as a provision. This is because there is a present obligation as a result of past events. It is probable that an outflow of resources / economic benefits will be required to settle the obligation and a reliable estimate can be made. The provision of £10,000 should be recognised as a liability in the statement of financial position with a corresponding expense shown in the statement of profit or loss.

Task 5.10

Richardson Logistics Ltd

a) Draft the statement of profit or loss and other comprehensive income for Richardson Logistics Ltd for the year ended year ended 31 March 20X2.

b) Draft the statement of financial position for Richardson Logistics Ltd year ended 31 March 20X2.

Use the workings boxes to help you.

Richardson Logistics Ltd Statement of Profit or Loss and Other Comprehensive Income for the year ended 31 March 20X2	
	£000
Revenue	34,876
Cost of Sales	-21,380
Gross profit	13,496
Distribution Costs	-3,216
Administrative Expenses	-5,666
Operating profit	4,614
Finance Costs	-256
Profit before tax	4,358
Tax	-372
Profit for the period from continuing operations	3,986
Other Comprehensive Income	2,700
Total comprehensive income for the year	6,686

Workings boxes:

Cost of Sales	£000
Opening Inventories	3,760
Purchases	20,984
Closing Inventories	-3,364
Total	21,380

Distribution Costs	£000
Distribution Costs	2,952
Storage costs	200
Accrual	64
Total	3,216

Administration Expenses	£000
Administration Expenses	5,824
Storage costs	-200
Irrecoverable debt	42
Total	5,666

Tax	£000
Current year	440
Previous year	-68
Total	372

Richardson Logistics Ltd Statement of Financial Position as at 31 March 20X2	
	£000
ASSETS	
Non-Current Assets	
Property, Plant and Equipment	21,284
Current Assets	
Inventories	3,364
Trade and Other Receivables	2,998
Cash and Cash Equivalents	224
TOTAL ASSETS	27,870
EQUITY AND LIABILITIES	
Equity	
Share Capital	12,960
Retained Earnings	5,542
Revaluation Reserve	2,700
Total Equity	21,202
Non-current Liabilities	
Bank loans	3,600
Current Liabilities	
Trade and Other Payables	2,628
Tax Payable	440
Total Liabilities	6,668
TOTAL EQUITY AND LIABILITIES	27,870

Trade and Other Receivables	£000
Trade and other receivables	2,716
Prepayment	324
Irrecoverable debt	-42
Total	2,998

Trade and Other Payables	£000
Trade and other payables	2,564
Accrual	64
Total	2,628

Chapter 6: Statement of Cash Flows - Answers

Task 6.1

Identify from the following options the purpose of the Statement of Cash Flows.

	✓
Profitability of the business over the period	
Financial strength of the business other the period	
How well the business has managed its cash resources over the period	✓
How the ownership of the business has changed over the period	

Task 6.2

Identify which of the following statements are true.

	✓
The Statement of Cash Flows is prepared on an accruals basis.	
The Statement of Cash Flows looks at the amount of money actually received and spent by the business.	✓
The Statement of Cash Flows is prepared on a cash basis.	✓
The Statement of Cash Flows looks at the amount of money expected to the received and spent by the business.	

Task 6.3

a) Complete the following sentences.

Choose from: goods or services, profit, ordinary course of business, trading profit.

The purpose of the reconciliation is to calculate the ***profit*** we have made through the ***ordinary course of business*** from the selling of ***goods or services***. This is also known as ***trading profit*** of the business.

b) Identify which of the following are added or deducted in the reconciliation of profit to net cash.

	Add / deduct
Depreciation	**Add**
Dividends received	**Deduct**
A gain on the disposal of PPE	**Deduct**
A loss on the disposal of PPE	**Add**
An increase in inventory	**Deduct**
A decrease in inventory	**Add**
An increase in receivables	**Deduct**
A decrease in receivables	**Add**
An increase in payables	**Add**
A decrease in payables	**Deduct**

Task 6.4

Identify if the following items are cash inflows or outflows.

	Inflow / outflow
Purchase of non-current assets	**Outflow**
Receipt of dividends	**Inflow**
Issue of new share capital	**Inflow**
Payment of dividends	**Outflow**
Taking out new bank loans	**Inflow**
Disposal of non-current assets	**Inflow**
Repayment of bank loans	**Outflow**

Task 6.5

Identify under which section the following items will appear in the Statement of Cash Flows.

Items	Heading
Purchase of non-current assets	**Investing**
Receipt of dividends	**Investing**
Issue of new share capital	**Financing**
Payment of dividends	**Financing**
Taking out or repayment new bank loans	**Financing**
Disposal of non-current assets	**Investing**

Task 6.6

Calculate how much Apollo Ltd have **actually paid** in regard to tax and interest during the year.

	Taxation	Interest
Balance at start of year	£19,300	£3,296
Charge for year (from P&L)	£15,820	£3,724
Balance at end of year	-£17,180	-£3,724
Amount Paid	£17,940	£3,296

Task 6.7

a) Prepare the reconciliation of profit before tax to net cash from operating activities for Parison Ltd for the year ended 31 December 20X5.

b) Prepare the Statement of Cash Flows for Parison Ltd for the year ended 31 December 20X5.

Reconciliation of profit before tax to net cash from operating activities	
	£000
Profit Before Tax	876
Adjustments for:	
Depreciation *(add on)*	380
Gain on disposal of PPE *(take off)*	-20
Dividends received *(take off)*	-40
Finance Costs *(add on)*	46
Adjustment in respect of inventories *(decrease - more cash)*	38
Adjustment in respect of trade receivables *(increase - less cash)*	-576
Adjustment in respect of trade payables *(increase - more cash)*	28
Cash generated by operations	732
Tax paid *(take off)*	-212
Interest paid *(take off)*	-46
Net cash from operating activities	474

Workings box

Tax paid	£000
Balance b/d	212
SPL charge	250
Balance c/d	-250
Total	212

Parison Ltd – Statement of Cash Flows for the year ended 31 December 20X5	
	£000
Net cash from operating activities	474
Investing Activities	
Dividend Received	40
Proceeds on Disposal	180
Purchases of PPE	-680
Net cash used in investing activities	-460
Financing Activities	
Repayment of bank loans	-200
Proceeds from shares issued	490
Dividend paid	-80
Net cash from financing activities	210
Net increase / decrease in cash and cash equivalents	224
Cash and cash equivalents at the beginning of the year	20
Cash and cash equivalents at the end of the year	244

Workings box

Purchases of PPE	£000
PPE at start of year	2,020
Depreciation charge	-380
Carrying amount of PPE sold	-160
Revaluation	200
PPE at end of year	-2,360
Total PPE additions	-£680

Note: Remember that your net increase or decrease in cash and cash equivalents should balance with the difference in cash and cash equivalents at the start and the end of the year. (£20,000 start of year + £224,000 increase = £244,000 end of year.)

Task 6.8

a) Prepare the reconciliation of profit before tax to net cash from operating activities for Rampage Ltd for the year ended 31 December 20X6.

b) Prepare the Statement of Cash Flows for Rampage Ltd for the year ended 31 December 20X6.

Reconciliation of profit before tax to net cash from operating activities	
	£000
Profit Before Tax	1,314
Adjustments for:	
Depreciation	570
Gain on disposal of PPE	-30
Dividends received	-60
Finance Costs	69
Adjustment in respect of inventories	57
Adjustment in respect of trade receivables	-864
Adjustment in respect of trade payables	42
Cash generated by operations	1,098
Tax paid	-318
Interest paid	-69
Net cash from operating activities	711

Workings box

Tax paid	£000
Balance b/d	318
SPL charge	375
Balance c/d	-375
Total	318

Rampage Ltd – Statement of Cash Flows for the year ended 31 December 20X6	
	£000
Net cash from operating activities	711
Investing Activities	
Dividend Received	60
Proceeds on Disposal	270
Purchases of PPE	-1,020
Net cash used in investing activities	-690
Financing Activities	
Repayment of bank loans	-300
Proceeds from shares issued	735
Dividend paid	-120
Net cash from financing activities	315
Net increase / decrease in cash and cash equivalents	336
Cash and cash equivalents at the beginning of the year	30
Cash and cash equivalents at the end of the year	366

Workings box

Purchases of PPE	£000
PPE at start of year	3,030
Depreciation charge	-570
Carrying amount of PPE sold	-240
Revaluation	300
PPE at end of year	-3,540
Total PPE additions	-1,020

Task 6.9

a) Prepare the reconciliation of profit before tax to net cash from operating activities for Roberts Ltd for the year ended 31 December 20X3.

b) Prepare the Statement of Cash Flows for Roberts Ltd for the year ended 31 December 20X3.

Reconciliation of profit before tax to net cash from operating activities	
	£000
Profit Before Tax	42,470
Adjustments for:	
Depreciation	4,810
Loss on disposal of PPE	58
Dividends received	-154
Finance Costs	68
Adjustment in respect of inventories	-488
Adjustment in respect of trade receivables	2,550
Adjustment in respect of trade payables	-8,686
Cash generated by operations	40,628
Tax paid	-2,120
Interest paid	-68
Net cash from operating activities	38,440

Workings box

Tax paid	£000
Balance b/d	2,120
SPL charge	1,958
Balance c/d	-1,958
Total	2,120

Roberts Ltd – Statement of Cash Flows for the year ended 31 December 20X3	
	£000
Net cash from operating activities	38,440
Investing Activities	
Dividend Received	154
Proceeds on Disposal	662
Purchases of PPE	-44,286
Net cash used in investing activities	-43,470
Financing Activities	
Repayment of bank loans	-2,800
Proceeds from shares issued	6,000
Dividend paid	-1,930
Net cash from financing activities	1,270
Net increase / decrease in cash and cash equivalents	-3,760
Cash and cash equivalents at the beginning of the year	4,952
Cash and cash equivalents at the end of the year	1,192

Workings box

Purchases of PPE	£000
PPE at start of year	56,944
Depreciation charge	-4,810
Carrying amount of PPE sold	-720
PPE at end of year	-95,700
Total PPE additions	-44,286

c) Prepare the Statement of Change in Equity for Roberts Ltd for the year ended 31 December 20X3.

	Share Capital	Share Premium	Revaluation Reserve	Retained Earnings	Total Equity
	£000	£000	£000	£000	£000
Balance at start of year	32,600	5,600		28,374	66,574
Changes in Equity:					
Comprehensive Income				40,512	40,512
Dividends				-1,930	-1,930
Issue of Share Capital	4,400	1,600			6,000
Balance at end of year	37,000	7,200	0	66,956	111,156

Task 6.10

a) Prepare the reconciliation of profit before tax to net cash from operating activities for Mercia Ltd for the year ended 31 December 20X3.

b) Prepare the Statement of Cash Flows for Mercia Ltd for the year ended 31 December 20X3.

Reconciliation of profit before tax to net cash from operating activities	
	£000
Profit Before Tax	1,752
Adjustments for:	
Depreciation	760
Gain on disposal of PPE	-40
Dividends received	-80
Finance Costs	92
Adjustment in respect of inventories	76
Adjustment in respect of trade receivables	-1,152
Adjustment in respect of trade payables	56
Cash generated by operations	1,464
Tax paid	-424
Interest paid	-92
Net cash from operating activities	948

Mercia Ltd – Statement of Cash Flows for the year ended 31 December 20X3	
	£000
Net cash from operating activities	948
Investing Activities	
Dividend Received	80
Proceeds on Disposal	360
Purchases of PPE	-1,360
Net cash used in investing activities	-920
Financing Activities	
Repayment of bank loans	-400
Proceeds from shares issued	980
Dividend paid	-160
Net cash from financing activities	420
Net increase / decrease in cash and cash equivalents	448
Cash and cash equivalents at the beginning of the year	40
Cash and cash equivalents at the end of the year	488

c) Prepare the Statement of Change in Equity for Mercia Ltd for the year ended 31 December 20X3.

	Share Capital	Share Premium	Revaluation Reserve	Retained Earnings	Total Equity
	£000	£000	£000	£000	£000
Balance at start of year	4,000	1,080		440	5,520
Changes in Equity:					
Comprehensive Income			400	1,252	1,652
Dividends				-160	-160
Issue of Share Capital	800	180			980
Balance at end of year	4,800	1,260	400	1,532	7,992

Chapter 7: Consolidated Accounts - Answers

Task 7.1

a) Identify which of the following statements are true.

	✓
Each individual company within a group must prepare individual financial statements.	✓
Consolidated financial statements need only be prepared when the parent company owns more than 75% of the subsidiary.	
Any intra-group transactions should be eliminated from the consolidated financial statements.	✓
When the parent has bought from, or sold to, a subsidiary, any unrealised profit on goods held in inventory at the year-end must be eliminated.	✓

b) Calculate the figure will be included for trade receivables in the consolidated Statement of Financial Position?

£185,000

Task 7.2

a) Calculate the net assets acquired.

Net Assets	£000
Share capital	400
Retained earnings	360
Total	760

b) Calculate the goodwill.

Goodwill	£000
Consideration	800
NCI at acquisition	190
Net assets acquired	-760
Impairment	-10
Goodwill	220

Task 7.3

Calculate the consolidated cost of sales to go in the consolidated Statement of Profit or Loss, after the necessary adjustments have been made?

	£
Consolidated cost of sales	**420,000**
Less intra-company transactions	**-65,000**
Unrealised profits	**9,000**
Total	**364,000**

Task 7.4

Prepare the consolidated statement of financial position for the group for the year ended 31 August 20X9.

Net Assets	**£000**
Subsidiary's Share Capital	**2,550**
Subsidiary's Retained earnings *(pre-acquisition)*	**1,200**
Adjustment to fair value *(revaluation)*	**200**
Net Assets	**3,950**

Goodwill	**£000**
Consideration (amount paid for the company)	**4,940**
NCI's share of net assets at acquisition *(3,950 x 20%)*	**790**
Less – Value of **net assets** (working box above)	**-3,950**
Goodwill	**1,780**
Less – Any impairments *(1,780 x 10%)*	**-178**
New Goodwill	**1,602**

Retained Earnings	**£000**
100% Parents Retained Earnings	**11,292**
% of Retained earnings attributable to the parent – post acquisition *(1,800 – 1,200 = 600 x 80%)*	**480**
Less – Any impairments	**-178**
Retained Earnings	**11,594**

Non-controlling Interest	£000
% of Share Capital attributable to NCI *(2,300 x 20%)*	**460**
% of Share Premium attributable to NCI *(250 x 20%)*	**50**
% of Retained Earnings attributable to NCI *(1,800 x 20%)*	**360**
% of Revaluation attributable to NCI *(200 x 20%)*	**40**
NCI	**910**

Harry Group Consolidated Statement of Financial Position		
	£000	***Workings***
Assets:		
Goodwill	**1,602**	*See workings*
Non-currents Assets	**13,627**	*10,312 + 3,115 + 200*
Current Assets:		
Inventories	**2,549**	*2,132 + 417*
Trade and other receivables	**8,428**	*6,668 + 1,780 - 20*
Cash and cash equivalents	**1,750**	*1,150 + 600*
Total Assets	**27,956**	
Equity and Liabilities:		
Equity:		
Share Capital	**6,000**	*100% parent*
Share Premium	**2,000**	*100% parent*
Retained Earnings	**11,594**	*See workings*
NCI	**910**	*See workings*
Total Equity	**20,504**	
Non-current liabilities	**700**	*600 + 100*
Current liabilities:		
Trade payables	**4,242**	*3,210 + 1,052 - 20*
Tax liability	**2,510**	*2,100 + 410*
Total Liabilities	**7,452**	
Total equity and liabilities	**27,956**	

Task 7.5

Prepare the consolidated statement of financial position for the group for the year ended 31st December 20X6. Enter whole numbers only.

Net Assets	£000
Subsidiary's Share Capital	**4,300**
Subsidiary's Retained earnings (pre-acquisition)	**1,230**
Adjustment to fair value (revaluation)	**1,000**
Net Assets	**6,530**

Goodwill	£000
Consideration (amount paid for the company)	**10,750**
NCI's share of net assets at acquisition	**1,959**
Less – Value of **net assets** (working box above)	**-6,530**
Goodwill	**6,179**
Less – Any impairments	**-130**
New Goodwill	**6,049**

Retained Earnings	£000
100% Parents Retained Earnings	**24,377**
% of Retained earnings attributable to the parent – post acquisition *(1,607 – 40 PUP) – 1,230 = 337 x 70%)*	**236**
Less – Any impairments	**-130**
Retained Earnings	**24,483**

Non-controlling Interest	£000
% of Share Capital attributable to NCI *(4,000 x 30%)*	**1,200**
% of Share Premium attributable to NCI *(300 x 30%)*	**90**
% of Retained Earnings attributable to NCI *(1,607 – 40) x 30%)*	**470**
% of Revaluation attributable to NCI *(1,000 x 30%)*	**300**
NCI	**2,060**

Jules Group Consolidated Statement of Financial Position		
	£000	***Workings***
Assets:		
Goodwill	**6,049**	*See workings*
Non-currents Assets	**29,427**	*24,312 + 4,115 + 1,000*
Current Assets:		
Inventories	**4,709**	*4,132 + 617 – 40 PUP*
Trade and other receivables	**10,373**	*7,113 + 3,260*
Cash and cash equivalents	**3,860**	*2,700 + 1,160*
Total Assets	**54,418**	
Equity and Liabilities:		
Equity:		
Share Capital	**10,000**	*100% parent*
Share Premium	**4,000**	*100% parent*
Retained Earnings	**24,483**	*See workings*
NCI	**2,060**	*See workings*
Total Equity	**40,543**	
Non-current liabilities	**1,710**	*1,400 + 310*
Current liabilities:		
Trade payables	**8,765**	*6,430 + 2,335*
Tax liability	**3,400**	*2,800 + 600*
Total Liabilities	**13,875**	
Total equity and liabilities	**54,418**	

Task 7.6

Prepare the consolidated statement of financial position for the group for the year ended 31st December 20X3.

Net Assets	£000
Subsidiary's Share Capital	**10,000**
Subsidiary's Retained earnings (pre-acquisition)	**860**
Adjustment to fair value (revaluation)	**400**
Net Assets	**11,260**

Goodwill	£000
Consideration (amount paid for the company)	**12,000**
NCI's share of net assets at acquisition	**2,252**
Less – Value of **net assets** (working box above)	**-11,260**
Goodwill	**2,992**
Less – Any impairments	**-40**
New Goodwill	**2,952**

Retained Earnings	£000
100% Parents Retained Earnings *(11,626 – 100 PUP)*	**11,526**
% of Retained earnings attributable to the parent – post acquisition *(1,360 – 860 = 500 x 80%)*	**400**
Less – Any impairments	**-40**
Retained Earnings	**11,886**

Non-controlling Interest	£000
% of Share Capital attributable to NCI *(10,000 x 20%)*	**2,000**
% of Retained Earnings attributable to NCI *(1,360 x 20%)*	**272**
% of Revaluation attributable to NCI *(400 x 20%)*	**80**
NCI	**2,352**

Doc Group Consolidated Statement of Financial Position		
	£000	***Workings***
Assets:		
Goodwill	**2,952**	*See workings*
Non-currents Assets	**27,740**	*21,600 + 5,740 + 400*
Current Assets:		
Inventories	**9,932**	*7,772 + 2,260 – 100 PUP*
Trade and other receivables	**18,668**	*13,528 + 5,140*
Cash and cash equivalents	**4,680**	*3,380 + 1,300*
Total Assets	**63,972**	
Equity and Liabilities:		
Equity:		
Share Capital	**36,000**	*100% parent*
Retained Earnings	**11,886**	*See workings*
NCI	**2,352**	*See workings*
Total Equity	**50,238**	
Non-current liabilities	**4,600**	*4,400 + 1,200 – 1,000*
Current liabilities:		
Trade payables	**7,534**	*5,894 + 1,640*
Tax liability	**1,600**	*1,360 + 240*
Total Liabilities	**13,534**	
Total equity and liabilities	**63,972**	

Task 7.7

Prepare the consolidated Statement of Profit or Loss for the group for the year ended 31st August 20X8.

Consolidated Statement of Profit or Loss	£	*Workings*
Revenue	**665,200**	*460,000+205,200*
Cost of Sales	**-275,920**	*179,120 + 96,800*
Gross Profit	**389,280**	
Other income	-	
Operating expenses	**-203,600**	*150,000 + 53,600*
Profit before tax	**185,680**	
Tax	**-43,808**	*33,288 + 10,520*
Profit for the period from continuing operations	**141,872**	
Attributable to:		
Equity holders of the parent	**133,016**	*141,872-8,856*
Non-controlling interests	**8,856**	**44,280 x 20%*

* Only the profit of the subsidiary is used. The subsidiary has no right to a percentage of the parent's profit.

Revenue	£
Andy	**460,000**
Red	**205,200**
Total	**665,200**

COS	£
Andy	**179,120**
Red	**96,800**
Total	**275,920**

Task 7.8

Prepare the consolidated Statement of Profit or Loss for the group for the year ended 31st March 20X8.

Consolidated Statement of Profit or Loss	£000
Revenue	**285,900**
Cost of Sales	**-121,880**
Gross Profit	**164,020**
Other income	-
Operating expenses	**-18,400**
Profit before tax	**145,620**

The inter-company transaction is £560,000. £560,000 - £360,000 = £200,000 / 2 = £100,000 PUP. The PUP will be added to the COS.

Revenue	£000
Consolidated revenue prior to adjustments *(197,260 + 89,200)*	**286,460**
Consolidation adjustment *(560 intercompany transaction)*	**-560**
Total	**285,900**

Cost of Sales	£000
Consolidated COS prior to adjustments *(97,740 + 24,600)*	**122,340**
Consolidation adjustment *(-560 + 100 PUP = -460)*	**-460**
Total	**121,880**

Task 7.9

Prepare the consolidated Statement of Profit or Loss for the group for the year ended 31st August 20X3.

Consolidated Statement of Profit or Loss	£000
Revenue	**32,700**
Cost of Sales	**-21,025**
Gross Profit	**11,675**
Other income	-
Operating expenses	**-5,149**
Profit before tax	**6,526**
Tax	**-1,545**
Profit for the period from continuing operations	**4,981**
Attributable to:	
Equity holders of the parent	**4,782**
Non-controlling interests *(1,990 x 10%)*	**199***

**(No PUP attributable to NCI when parent sells to subsidiary.)*

Revenue	£000
Consolidated revenue prior to adjustments *(21,000 + 12,000)*	**33,000**
Consolidation adjustment *(300 intercompany transaction)*	**-300**
Total	**32,700**

Cost of Sales	£000
Consolidated COS prior to adjustments *(14,100 + 7,175)*	**21,275**
Consolidation adjustment *(-300 + 50 PUP = -250)*	**-250**
Total	**21,025**

Task 7.10

Prepare the consolidated Statement of Profit or Loss for the group for the year ended 31st December 20X3.

Consolidated Statement of Profit or Loss	£000
Revenue	18,540
Cost of Sales	-7,800
Gross Profit	10,740
Other income	0
Operating expenses	-8,930
Profit before tax	1,810
Tax	-540
Profit for the period from continuing operations	1,270
Attributable to:	
Equity holders of the parent	1,000
Non-controlling interests *((1,410-60 PUP) x 20%)*	270

Revenue	£000
Consolidated revenue prior to adjustments *(12,600 + 6,300)*	18,900
Consolidation adjustment *(360 intercompany transaction)*	-360
Total	18,540

Cost of Sales	£000
Consolidated COS prior to adjustments *(5,400 + 2,700)*	8,100
Consolidation adjustment *(-360 + 60 PUP = -300)*	-300
Total	7,800

Goodwill	£000
Consolidated operating expenses prior to adjustments *(6,900 + 2,010)*	8,910
Consolidation adjustment *(200 x 10% = 20)*	20
Total	8,930

Chapter 8: Financial Ratios - Answers

Task 8.1

State the correct formulas for the following ratios.

Ratio	Formula
Return on capital employed	**Operating profit / total equity + non-current Liabilities x 100**
Trade payables collection period (days)	**Trade payables / cost of sales x 365**
Asset turnover (non- current assets)	**Revenue / non-current assets**
Trade receivables collection period (days)	**Trade receivables / revenue x 365**
Inventory holding period (days)	**Inventories / cost of sales x 365**
Working capital cycle	**Inventory days + receivable days – payable days**

Task 8.2

Calculate the following to two decimal places.

	%
Gross Profit Percentage	**58.77**
Operating Profit Percentage	**10.58**
Return on Capital Employed	**4.42**

Task 8.3

Calculate the following to two decimal places.

Gross Profit Percentage	**44.16**	%
Operating Profit Percentage	**19.20**	%
Gearing	**30.65**	%
Inventory turnover	**8.18**	times

Task 8.4

a) State the correct formulae for the following ratios.

Ratio	Formula
Current ratio	**Current assets / current liabilities**
Quick ratio / Acid test	**(Current assets – inventories) / current liabilities**
Inventory holding period (days)	**Inventories / cost of sales x 365**
Gearing ratio	**Non-current liabilities / (total equity + non-current liabilities) x100%**
Return on shareholder funds	**Profit after tax / Total Equity**
Inventory turnover	**Cost of sales / inventories**

b) Calculate the following ratios to TWO decimal places.

Current ratio	**1.16**	:1
Quick ratio / Acid test	**0.68**	:1
Inventory holding period (days)	**47.03**	days
Gearing ratio	**29.75**	%
Return on shareholder funds	**59.00**	%
Inventory turnover	**7.76**	times

Task 8.5

a) State the correct formulae for the following ratios.

Ratio	Formula
Return on capital employed	**Operating profit / total equity + non-current Liabilities x 100%**
Inventory holding period (days)	**Inventories / cost of sales x 365**
Trade receivables collection period (days)	**Trade receivables / revenue x 365**
Trade payables collection period (days)	**Trade payables / cost of sales x 365**
Working capital cycle	**Inventory days + receivable days – payable days**
Asset turnover (non- current assets)	**Revenue / non-current assets**

b) Calculate the following ratios to TWO decimal places.

Return on capital employed	**18.71**	%
Inventory holding period (days)	**71.53**	days
Trade receivables collection period (days)	**34.79**	days
Trade payables collection period (days)	**64.34**	days
Working capital cycle	**41.98**	days
Asset turnover (non - current assets)	**1.44**	times

Task 8.6

a) Complete the missing ratios in the scorecard to one decimal place where appropriate.

Scorecard for year ending the 30/09/20X5	JCD Ltd	Competitor
Gross profit %	62.7%	**63.2%**
Operating profit %	17.8%	**12.6 %**
ROCE	12.9%	**10.1 %**
Current ratio	2.2:1	**2.1:1**
Acid test	1.3:1	**1.1:1**
Inventory holding days	89 days	**106 days**
Trade receivables	42 days	**44 days**
Trade payables payment period	74 days	83 days
Working capital cycle	57 days	**67 days**

b) Based on the scorecard above, select the correct assumptions for the following.

Profitability	
The gross profit and operating profit percentages are better for the competitor, this indicates that the competitor has a better use of working capital.	
The ROCE of the competitor, in comparison to JCD Ltd, indicates that the competitor is using its working capital more efficiently.	
The overall profitability of JCD Ltd is better than the competitor. Although the gross profit percentage is slightly higher for the competitor, JCD Ltd may have lower operating costs and uses its working capital more efficiently.	✓

Liquidity	
The liquidity of the competitor is better. This indicates that company has a good short-term solvency.	
The liquidity of JCD Ltd is better. The current ratio indicates that the company has enough current assets to cover its current liabilities. The quick ratio / acid test is a better test of liquidity as it shows the immediate solvency of a company because inventories are less liquid.	✓
The current ratio of both companies is a cause for concern and should be below 1:1, which is also the industry average.	

Working capital cycle	
The working capital cycle for the competitor is considerably better than JCD Ltd. This could be due the better inventory holding days.	
The working capital cycle for JCD Ltd is better than the competitor. This indicates that the amount of time between paying for materials and receiving the cash for the sold goods is quicker than that of the competitor. This could be due to the better inventory holding period.	✓
The competitor has a better working capital cycle of 21 days. This indicates that the competitor making better use of its resources and has a better turnaround of inventory.	

Overall performance	
The overall performance of the competitor is better than JCD Ltd. This indicates that JCD Ltd should reduce its selling prices to gain more customers.	
The overall performance of the competitor is significantly worse than JCD Ltd. The current ratios show serious cause for concern and liquidity issues.	
The overall performance of the competitor is slightly worse than JCD Ltd. Whilst this is good, there are limitations on the accuracy of the ratios as we can only assume what has affected these. JCD Ltd should still attempt to improve its ratios and complete another comparison/review in the near future to identify any significant changes.	✓

Task 8.7

Consider the following ratios and state whether the position has got better or worse from the previous year.

Ratio	20X4	20X3	Better	Worse
Inventory holding days	56 days	45 days		✓
Current ratio	2.3:1	2:1	✓	
Gearing	45%	52%	✓	
Trade receivable days	42 days	36 days		✓
Interest cover	3 times	2.5 times	✓	
ROCE	24.7%	32.2%		✓

Task 8.8

a) For each of the following ratios:

i) Identify whether the ratio in 20X3 is better or worse in comparison to 20X2.

ii) Explain what the ratios tell you about the performance and efficiency of the company.

Gross Profit Margin

	✓
Better	
Worse	✓

Comments

The gross profit margin has fallen. This means that the company is making less profit on each unit sold.

This could have been caused by an increase in material or production costs, this would cause gross profit percentage to fall.

Alternatively, the selling price may have been reduced to attract more customers or a change in the mix of products sold.

Operating Profit Margin

	✓
Better	✓
Worse	

Comments

The operating profit percentage has improved in comparison to 20X2. This means that more operating profit is being generated from sales.

This ratio shows us how well the business is controlling its costs. This could indicate that the operating expenses may have decreased and that the company has managed to reduce its operating expenses from the previous year. Alternatively, selling prices may have increased from the previous year.

Trade Receivables Collection Period

	✓
Better	
Worse	✓

Comments

The trade receivables collection period has worsened in comparison to 20X2. This could mean that customers are taking longer to pay. This could be due to customers having extended or over generous credit terms or it may be due to credit control procedures being inadequate or due to irrecoverable debts.

Inventory Holding Period

	✓
Better	
Worse	✓

Comments

Inventory holding period has deteriorated in comparison to 20X2. The company is taking longer to convert inventory into cash. This shows that the company may not be managing inventory as efficiently as it did the previous year. Long holding periods could be an indication of old or obsolete inventory and the business could be incurring unnecessary storage costs. If selling prices have increased this may make it more difficult to sell the inventory and reduce demand. Reduced marketing expenditure could also lead to a reduction in demand, this could be consistent with the operating profit margin as this indicates that operating overheads have been reduced.

b) Make <u>one</u> recommendation on how to improve each of the ratios given.

Gross Profit Margin

To improve the gross profit percentage the company could increase the selling price or reduce production costs. Increasing the selling price may be off putting to customers and decrease demand, therefore it may be a safer option to try and source raw materials at a lower price.

Operating Profit Margin

This ratio might improve if operating expenses were reduced. As the operating profit percentage has already improved it seems unlikely costs will be able to be reduced significantly.

Trade Receivables Period

The trade receivable collection days have increased so credit control procedures should be reviewed to ensure payments are received on time and customers are credit checked before offering credit terms.

Inventory Holding Period

Management may need to improve ordering procedures to ensure high levels of inventory are not sat redundantly in the warehouse and 'tying up cash'.

**Other valid points might be applicable.*

Task 8.9

a) For each of the following ratios:

i) Identify whether the ratio in 20X4 is better or worse in comparison to 20X3.

ii) Explain what the ratios tell you about the performance and efficiency of the company.

Gross Profit Margin

	✓
Better	✓
Worse	

Comments

The gross profit margin has increased by 6%. This means more gross profit is being generated on sales. This could have been caused by a change in product mix, a higher selling price or a reduction in production costs.

Operating Profit Margin

	✓
Better	
Worse	✓

Comments

The operating profit percentage decreased by 8%. This means that less operating profit is being generated from sales. This could have been caused by a decrease in sales or an increase in costs or even a mixture of both. Due to the improvement of the gross profit percentage, we could assume this may be due to an increase in operating expenses.

Return on Capital Employed

	✓
Better	
Worse	✓

Comments

The return on capital employed has decreased by 8%.

This means that less net profit is being generated from capital employed. This means that the capital is working less efficiently in terms of generating profit. This could be due to lower profits, higher equity or higher non-current liabilities. This is consistent with the deteriorating interest cover ratio.

Gearing

	✓
Better	
Worse	✓

Comments

The gearing ratio has increase by 12.5%. This could mean that the company has taken out additional loans during the year. Whilst this a good indication that the bank is willing to lend to the company, this could also cause issues with raising finance in the future as the company could appear more risky.

Interest Cover

	✓
Better	
Worse	✓

Comments

The interest ratio has worsened by 2.5 times. This means there is less operating profit to cover interest payments. The increase in interest cover could relate to the increase in possible new loans taken out during the year. During 20X3 the company could cover the interest payments 5.1 times over from the operating profit however, the company can only do this 2.6 times for 20X4. This will mean that the company will appear more risky to potential lenders as this has almost halved over the year.

b) What advice would you give to the board of the company.

The gross profit margin has increased but the operating profit margin has fallen. This means the company needs to review its operating expenses and gain better control of them. This could then improve the interest cover ratio and then the company would appear less risky. The company should also look at its financing structure and try to improve the gearing ratio. If the company has a high gearing ratio then the company could struggle to gain finance in the future and could be off putting to potential investors.

Task 8.10

a) For each of the following ratios:

i) Identify whether the ratio in 20X7 is better or worse in comparison to 20X6.

ii) Explain what the ratios tell you about the performance and efficiency of the company.

iii) What may have caused the change in performance? Give one reason.

Inventory Holding Period

	✓
Better	✓
Worse	

Comments

The inventory holding period decreased 4 days from 20X6 to 20X7. This means that inventory is held for a shorter period from the time of purchase or production of goods to when they are sold. This could be an indication of improved control or management of inventory.

This could be due to the company is only purchasing or producing inventory that is ordered from customers and therefore able to be sold fairly quickly. Another possible reason could be that the company has written off or disposed of obsolete or old stock. This would ensure that any stock held is able to be sold and this in turn will reduce the inventory holding period.

Trade Receivables Collection Period

	✓
Better	✓
Worse	

Comments

The trade receivable collection period has decreased by 8 days from 20X6 to 20X7. This means that the company is collecting money owed to them more quickly than it did in the previous year. This will improve cash flow, reduce time wasted by chasing customers for payment and reduce any potential bank charges or interest costs should the company need to use a finance facility until payment is received (i.e. overdraft).

A possible reason for this is that the company has introduced more effective credit control procedures. These could include reviewing or enforcing credit terms of customers, chasing customers, running credit checks on customers or encouraging customer to pay more quickly with the advantage of prompt payment discounts.

Trade Payables Payment Period

	✓
Better	✓
Worse	

Comments

The trade payables collection period has increased from 40 days in 20X6 to 45 days in 20X7. This is an improvement of 7 days.

An increase in trade payables collection period is seen as beneficial to a company as it is using free credit to finance the company, without any interest charges etc.

This could mean that Imagine Products Ltd has made an agreement with its suppliers to increase the credit terms which would allow the company a longer amount of days to pay.

In contrast, this could mean that the company may have cash flow problems and it has not been unable to pay suppliers on time and within the credit terms. If this is the case, this could cause problems for the company because suppliers may refuse to make further sales to the company or expect the company to pay upfront in the future. The reputation and the credit rating of the business could also be affected.

Working Capital Cycle

	✓
Better	✓
Worse	

Comments

The working capital cycle has improved by 16 days. The working capital cycle shows how long it takes from the purchase of inventory from the supplier, to when the company receives payment from its customer. This time should be as short as possible.

The working capital cycle has fallen from 46 days in 20X6 to 30 days in 20X7. This means that the company is managing its working capital more efficiently than it was in 20X6. The period of time between paying for the inventory to when the company receives payment for the items has been reduced by 16 days. A possible reason for this (looking at the information above) is that this is a result of the customers paying more quickly, inventory is being managed more efficiently and the extended period the company is using to pay its suppliers have all had a positive effect on the working capital cycle.

c) Explain why using historical data may not always be a reliable basis for predicting financial performance.

Using historical data may not always be a reliable basis for predicting financial performance. Ratio analysis uses historical information. This means that the financial information provided is up to that point time, but is not current. This means the ratios are looking at the past and not the present. Ratio analysis does not consider external factors such as economic factors, recession and inflation or factors affecting specific industries.

Financial information can also be manipulated and can give a misleading representation of a business.

This page is left intentionally blank.

Mock Exam - Answers

Task 1 (23 marks)

a) Draft the statement of profit or loss and other comprehensive income for Ascot Ltd for the year ended 31st March 20X9.

Use the working boxes to help you.

Workings boxes:

Cost of Sales	£000
Opening Inventories	5,640
Purchases	48,900
Purchase returns	-766
Closing Inventories	-6,806
Total	46,968

Distribution Costs	£000
Distribution Costs	4,555
Accrual	120
Total	4,675

Administrative Expenses	£000
Administrative expenses	6,589
Prepayment	-96
Total	6,493

Ascot Ltd Statement of Profit or Loss and Other Comprehensive Income for the year ended 31st March 20X9	
	£000
Revenue	65,113
Cost of Sales	-46,968
Gross Profit	18,145
Distribution Costs	-4,675
Administration Expenses	-6,493
Profit from Operations	6,977
Finance Costs	-720
Profit Before Tax	6,257
Taxation	-2,540
Profit for the Year from Continuing Operations	3,717
Other Comprehensive Income for the Year	3,000
Total Comprehensive Income for the Year	6,717

c) Draft the Statement of Financial Position for Ascot Ltd as at 31st March 20X9.

ASSETS	£000
Non-Current Assets	
Property Plant and Equipment	29,380
Current Assets	
Inventories	6,806
Trade and Other Receivables	4,663
Cash and Cash Equivalents	3,519
	14,988
Total Assets	44,368
EQUITY AND LIABILITIES	
Equity	
Share Capital	14,000
Retained Earnings	9,467
Revaluation Reserve	3,000
Total Equity	26,467
Non-Current Liabilities	
Bank Loans	12,000
	12,000
Current Liabilities	
Trade and Other Payables	3,361
Tax Liability	2,540
	5,901
Total Liabilities	17,901
Total Equity and Liabilities	44,368

Working boxes:

Property, Plant and Equipment	
	£000
PPE at cost	55,360
Accumulated Depreciation	-28,980
Revaluation	3,000
Total	29,380

Trade and Other Receivables	
	£000
Trade Receivables	4,567
Prepayments	96
Total	4,663

Trade and Other Payables	
	£000
Trade and other Payables	2,642
Accruals	239
Accrual – Finance Costs	360
Accrual – Distribution Costs	120
Total	3,361

Retained Earnings	
	£000
Retained Earnings @ 01/04/20X8	6,590
Profit for the Year	3,717
Dividends Paid	-840
Total	9,467

b) Draft the Statement of Changes in Equity for Ascot Ltd for the year ended 31st March 20X9.

	Share Capital	Revaluation	Retained Earnings	Total Equity
	£000	**£000**	**£000**	**£000**
Balance at 1st April 20X8	14,000	0	6,590	20,590
Changes in Equity				
Total Comprehensive Income		3,000	3,717	6,717
Dividends			-840	-840
Balance at 31st March 20X9	14,000	3,000	9,467	26,467

Task 2 (17 marks)

a) Complete the following workings boxes to calculate the correct figures for Proceeds on Disposal of PPE and Purchases of PPE.

Proceeds on Disposal of PPE	
	£000
Carrying amount of PPE sold	823
Gain / Loss on disposal of PPE	-40
	783

Purchases of PPE	
	£000
PPE at start of year	140,950
Depreciation Charge	-14,390
Carrying amount of PP sold	-823
PPE at end of year	-208,950
Total PPE additions	-83,213

b) Prepare a reconciliation of profit before tax to net cash from operating activities for Garibaldi Ltd for the year ended 31st December 20X9.

	£000
Profit before tax	59,167
Adjustments For:	
Depreciation	14,390
Gain / Loss on disposal of PPE	40
Dividends received	-154
Finance Costs	2,106
Adjustment in respect of inventories	1,213
Adjustment in respect of trade receivables	1,739
Adjustment in respect of trade payables	1,390
Cash Generated by Operations	79,891
Interest Paid	-2,106
Taxation Paid	-8,862
Net Cash from Operating Activities	68,923

c) Prepare the Statement of Cash Flows for Garibaldi Ltd for the year ended 31st December 20X9.

	£000
Net Cash From Operating Activities	**68,923**
Investing Activities	
Purchases of PPE	**-83,213**
Proceeds on Disposal of PPE	**783**
Dividends Received	**154**
Investment	**-10,500**
Net Cash Used in Investing Activities	**-92,776**
Financing Activities	
Increase in share capital	**2,895**
Increase in loan	**2,400**
Dividends paid	**-1,800**
Net Cash From Financing Activities	**3,495**
Net increase / (decrease) in cash and cash equivalents	**-20,358**
Cash and cash equivalents at beginning of year	**6,390**
Cash and cash equivalents at end of year	**-13,968**

Task 3 (8 marks)

a) Identify the two primary users of published financial statements, and, for each, explain the ways in which they will use them.

Investors (both current and potential) are primarily interested in the profitability of the business, as they will be deciding whether or not to invest in the company. Ratios such as Return on Capital Employed and Return on Shareholder Funds are useful in comparing different companies.

Lenders are more concerned with the liquidity of the company, as they are primarily concerned with ensuring that any existing loans can be repaid in line with the agreed terms. Profitability is also a concern, particularly if the lender is considering lending more money to the entity.

b) Explain the importance of the fundamental ethical concepts of Integrity and Professional Competence and Due Care when preparing financial statements.

Integrity – financial statements should be prepared with openness and honesty. Any figures or valuations included in the statements should reflect a true and fair view. This includes not understating income or overstating expenses to manipulate profit (e.g. to pay less tax) or in valuing inventories or non-current assets.

Acting with Professional Competence means that accountants should only carry out work for which they have been properly trained and for which they have appropriate experience. For example, an AAT Level 2 student should not prepare the financial statements for a limited company (although they can be involved in the process so long as they are suitably supervised).

Due care implies that the accountant should ensure that they have sufficient time and resources to complete the work, and should work to the highest standards at all time. Failure to do so may lead to errors or omissions which could have a material effect on the statements.

Task 4 (12 marks)

a) Explain (with reasons) whether this should be treated as a finance lease or a short-term lease, and how it should be shown in the financial statements of Jammy Ltd.

This appears to be a short-term lease, rather than a finance lease. Although some of the risks of ownership transferred to Jammy Ltd during the period of the lease, the nature of the transaction is more of a rental agreement – particularly because at the end of the period the ownership and control of the asset remained with the lessor (the lease company). Under IFRS 16 the lease payments should therefore be treated as an expense in the SPLOCI and the asset should not be recorded as such in the SFP of Jammy Ltd.

b) Making reference to the relevant International Accounting Standard, explain how this should be accounted for in the financial statements for the year ended 31st December 20X2.

Under IAS10, this would be classed as an adjusting event, as it refers to events which were in existence at the financial statements date (31st December 20X2). As such, the expense and liability arising from the court case (£45,000) should be included in the financial statements for the year ended 31st December 20X2) even though the final decision was not reached until after this date. An expense should be included in the SPLOCI, along with a corresponding provision/liability in the SFP.

c) Explain, with reference to the relevant International Accounting Standard, how the forthcoming expenditure should be accounted for.

According to IAS 38, most research and development expenditure is treated as an expense in the year it is incurred. However, the £1,190,000 expenditure on the new laboratory will be treated as capital expenditure as a new non-current asset is being created. The remaining expenditure can only be capitalised as development expenditure if it meets six criteria. It is unlikely that this expenditure can be capitalised, as it is far from certain that future economic benefits will arise for Jammy Ltd, nor that the project will even be completed. Therefore, this expenditure should be treated as an expense in the SPLOCI.

d) With reference to the relevant International Accounting Standard, identify whether the value of the machine has been impaired, and if so, how any impairment loss should be accounted for in the financial statements of Jammy Ltd.

IAS 36 requires entities to review assets which show signs of impairment. The carrying value is compared to the value in use (the discounted value of future cash flows) and the fair value less costs to sell. In this example, the carrying value is £155,000, the value in use is £150,000 and the fair value less costs to sell are £148,000. Because the carrying value is more than the higher of the other two, an impairment loss has occurred. The value of the impairment loss is £155,000 - £150,000 = £5,000. This should be credited to the non-current asset (reducing its value in the financial statements) and recorded as an expense in the SPLOCI.

e) Demonstrate how this transaction would be accounted for in the consolidated financial statements at 31st December 20X9.

There is an unrealised profit on these goods of 20% x (£38,000 - £23,000) = £3,000. This profit will only be realised when the goods are sold outside the group as a whole. There are two adjustments required; firstly, the sale (£38,000) should be eliminated from the group's sales and cost of sales calculations (to avoid double counting), and then the unrealised profit (£3,000) should be debited to Retained Earnings and credited to Inventory in the SFP.

Task 5 (30 marks)

Complete the following workings boxes to calculate the correct figures for Goodwill, Retained Earnings and Non-Controlling Interest.

Goodwill	
	£000
Consideration	**23,000**
Non-controlling Interest at acquisition *(31,640 x 40%)*	**12,656**
Less: Net assets acquired *(18,000 + 9,640 + 4,000)*	**-31,640**
Initial Goodwill	**4,016**
Less: Impairment Adjustment *(4,016 x 25%)*	**-1,004**
Adjusted Goodwill	**3,012**

Retained Earnings	
	£000
Rich Ltd	**22,526**
Tea Ltd attributable to Rich Ltd *(post acquisition retained earnings)*	**1,260**
Less: Impairment Adjustment	**-1,004**
	22,782

Non-Controlling Interest (NCI)	
	£000
Share Capital attributable to NCI *(12,000 x 40%)*	**4,800**
Share Premium *(6,000 x 40%)*	**2,400**
Retained Earnings *(11,740 x 40%)*	**4,696**
Revaluation Reserve *(4,000 x 40%)*	**1,600**
Non-Controlling Interest	**13,496**

Draft the Consolidated Statement of Financial Position for Rich Ltd as at 31st March 20X4.

ASSETS	**£000**
Non-Current Assets	
Goodwill	3,012
Property, Plant and Equipment	76,690
	79,702
Current Assets	
Inventories	25,672
Trade Receivables	13,360
Cash and Cash Equivalents	1,585
	40,617
Total Assets	120,319
EQUITY AND LIABILITIES	
Equity	
Share Capital	38,000
Share Premium	11,000
Retained Earnings	22,782
Non-Controlling Interest	13,496
Total Equity	85,278
Non-Current Liabilities	
Bank Loans	18,000
Current Liabilities	
Trade Payables	12,679
Taxation	4,362
	17,041
Total Liabilities	35,041
Total Equity and Liabilities	120,319

Task 6 (8 marks)

Calculate the following ratios to ONE decimal place:

Gross profit percentage	**46.0**	%
Operating profit percentage	**15.0**	%
ROCE	**20.9**	%
Asset turnover (net assets)	**1.4**	times

Task 7 (22 marks)

Prepare an email to your Jeremiah containing:

a) Whether the ratio is better or worse compared to the industry average and what it tells you about the performance of the company.

b) Based solely on the ratios given, what advice would you give to the investor (with reasons) as to whether the investor should buy the shares and invest in the company or not.

To: Jeremiah Bootfeather
From: AAT student
Subject: Investment in Cheesan Ltd.

Good afternoon Jeremiah

I have summarised below relevant ratios for Cheesan Ltd.

Gross profit ratio:

The gross profit ratio has improved. The gross profit margin has increased by 3.5%. This means more gross profit is being generated on sales. This could have been caused by a change in product mix, a higher selling price or a reduction in production costs.

Operating profit ratio:

In contrast to the gross profit ratio, the operating profit ratio has deteriorated. This means that less operating profit is being generated from sales. Normally, this could be due to reduced gross profit margin (but not in this case) or an increase in expenses. This ratio can also show us how well the business is controlling its costs. This could have been caused by a decrease in sales or an increase in costs or even a mixture of both. Due to the improvement of the gross profit percentage, we could assume this may be due to an increase in operating expenses.

Interest cover:

The interest cover ratio has deteriorated in comparison to the previous year. This shows that there is less profit available to meet the interest payments making the company appear more risky. The ratio may be lower due to lower operating profits. This could be due to higher interest payments or rates or the company may have more debt / non-current liabilities so the gearing ratio may also be high. This could make it difficult to obtain finance in the future. This can cause issues with cash flow and makes the company look more risky.

ROCE:

The return on capital employed has deteriorated in comparison to the previous year. This means that less profit is being generated by the capital employed. This suggests that capital is working less efficiently than it should. This could be due to lower profits or higher total equity (higher share capital, retained earnings or revaluation surplus) or higher non-current liabilities. Higher non-current liabilities would be the most likely cause as this coincides with the lower interest cover ratio. However, further investigate would be needed.

In conclusion, only the gross profit ratio has improved, whilst the other ratios have deteriorated. The ratios suggest that the investment is now much riskier than previously. Interest cover is a cause for concern. When all of the above is considered, along with the interest cover being worse too, the company is more risky, therefore it would not be wise to invest in the company at this time.

Kind regards

AAT Student